Foul Deeds & Suspicious Deaths in Bath

TRUE CRIME FROM WHARNCLIFFE

Foul Deeds and Suspicious Deaths Series

Staffordshire and The Potteries
Colchester
Manchester
Guilford
Derby
Northampton
Pontefract and Castleford
Tees
Bedford
Bristol
Carlisle
Newcastle
Southend-on-Sea
Barnsley
Birmingham
Blackburn and Hyndburn
Chesterfield
Coventry
Ealing
Guernsey
Huddersfield
Leeds
Liverpool
Newport
Nottingham
Rotherham
London's East End
Wigan
More Foul Deeds Wakefield
Mansfield
Leicester
Stratford and South Warwickshire
Brighton
Folkestone and Dover
Oxfordshire
Black Country
Durham
Bradford
Cambridge
Halifax
Scunthorpe
Barking, Dagenham & Chadwell Heath
Bath
More Foul Deeds Birmingham
Bolton
More Foul Deeds Chesterfield
Croydon
Grimsby
Hampstead, Holborn and St Pancras
Hull
Lewisham and Deptford
London's West End
Norfolk
Portsmouth
Warwickshire
York

OTHER TRUE CRIME BOOKS FROM WHARNCLIFFE

Norfolk Mayhem and Murder
The A-Z of London Murders
Unsolved Murders in Victorian and Edwardian London
Unsolved Yorkshire Murders
A-Z Yorkshire Murder
Brighton Crime and Vice 1800-2000
Essex Murders
Executions & Hangings in Newcastle and Morpeth
Norwich Murders
Unsolved Norfolk Murders
Yorkshire's Murderous Women
Black Barnsley
Durham Executions
Strangeways Hanged

Please contact us via any of the methods below for more information or a catalogue.

WHARNCLIFFE BOOKS
47 Church Street – Barnsley – South Yorkshire – S70 2AS
Tel: 01226 734555 – 734222 Fax: 01226 – 734438
E-mail: enquiries@pen-and-sword.co.uk
Website: www.wharncliffebooks.co.uk

Foul Deeds & Suspicious Deaths in

BATH

KIRSTEN ELLIOTT

Series Editor
Brian Elliott

Wharncliffe Books

First Published in Great Britain in 2007 by
Wharncliffe Books
an imprint of
Pen and Sword Books Ltd
47 Church Street
Barnsley
South Yorkshire
S70 2AS

ISBN: 978-184563-029-4

A CIP catalogue record for this book is available from the British Library.

Typeset in 10/12pt Plantin by Concept, Huddersfield.

Printed and bound in England by CPI UK.

Pen and Sword Books Ltd incorporates the Imprints of Pen & Sword Aviation, Pen & Sword Maritime, Pen & Sword Military, Wharncliffe Books, Pen & Sword Select, Pen and Sword Military Classics and Leo Cooper.

For a complete list of Pen & Sword titles please contact
PEN & SWORD BOOKS LIMITED
47 Church Street
Barnsley
South Yorkshire
S70 2BR
England
E-mail: enquiries@pen-and-sword.co.uk
Website: www.pen-and-sword.co.uk

Contents

Introduction

Visitors come to Bath mainly for its history and architecture. With the Roman Baths, the Georgian terraces, and a lively restaurant and pub culture, it offers them a welcome. It is marketed in many ways – Bath the Georgian City, the Floral City, even the City of Love. What the guidebooks do not say, however, is that it could equally be Bath the City of Crime – or at least Bath the City of Mysteries. In this book, we look at some of these dark or puzzling events. Many deal with death – by murder, manslaughter, or by the victim's own hand. Some turn out to be less exciting than first thought. For fiction writers, the city has also proved irresistible as a scenario for dark deeds, and for aficionados of the detective story, we look at some of the best crime novels set here. To whet your appetite, here's the story of the crime that got away.

Among the list of famous – perhaps that should be notorious – murders, the story of the Brides in the Bath ranks highly. What is not widely known is that the murderer had, appropriately perhaps, a Bath connection. The final Bride in the Bath, Margaret Lofty, was literally that, having made the fatal error of marrying her killer, George Smith, in the city. Smith, who operated under a number of aliases, was using the name John Lloyd when he came to stay in Bath in December 1914. He told the landlady that he needed a room for a young lady – the unfortunate Margaret Elizabeth Lofty, the daughter of a wealthy Bristol clergyman. She arrived on 15 December and they were married at Bath Registry Office, then situated at No. 3 North Parade. Had Smith decided to stay in the city, Bath might forever be connected with his activities, especially in view of the name which the popular press gave to the series of murders. Fortunately for the city's image, they caught a train to London and took lodgings in Holloway.

On 18 December, Margaret made a will in her husband's favour. By the evening she was dead, drowned in the bath. Although no suspicions were aroused at the time, the inquest was reported in the *News of the World*, together with a picture of 'John Lloyd'. An alert Blackpool lodging-house keeper spotted that Lloyd looked a lot like George Smith, whose wife Alice had also drowned in the bath, at his lodging-house. He wrote to the police – and the truth about Smith, also known as Henry Williams, came to light. Bessy Williams had been his first victim, followed by Alice, and then Margaret. All had drowned in their baths. He was also a serial bigamist, two previous

No. 3 North Parade – in 1914 this was Bath Registry Office, and here the unfortunate Margaret Lofty married George Smith. The Author

wives having escaped his bagnatorial attentions. He was hanged at Maidstone Gaol in August 1915.

During the investigations, another Bath connection came to light. At an earlier stage in his career, Smith had run a shop in Bath, during which time he had written several letters to the Bath Chronicle. They were on subjects such as the lack of probity in civic life, the decline of moral values among the young, hooliganism in the city, and the baleful effects of popular fiction. He would doubtless disapprove strongly of a book such as this, dealing as it does with morally dubious characters, mob violence, and an entire chapter on popular fiction. With a seal of disapproval like that, I hope you will feel impelled to read on.

Acknowledgements

As ever with my books based on research, I would like to thank the staff of Bath Central Library for their patience and assistance, as well as the ever-helpful Colin Johnston and his staff at Bath Record Office.

Thanks also go to Derek Stimpson and the Gunmakers' Company for assistance relating to the death of John Hanning Speke. I am indebted to them for information relating to shotguns and shooting practices of the mid-nineteenth century. Mr Stimpson provided the likely reconstruction of the cause of the shooting.

Finally, I would like to acknowledge the debt I owe to my late parents, Jean and Alan Fry – not just because they encouraged my interest in history, but also because, through their enjoyment of well-written, well-constructed crime fiction, I too came to enjoy this genre. The result is this book.

CHAPTER 1

Dark Deeds and Dark Ages

A catalogue of mysteries from Bath's earliest days

The Hot Springs of Bath have attracted human beings ever since the Stone Age. And where there are human beings there is human nature – with its light and its dark sides. When did the first theft or the first murder take place in the valley which became Bath? Did some primitive hunter, hungry after a bad day's hunting, steal a bone from a more fortunate fellow? And did that hunter, in rage, pick up his flint-tipped spear and run it through the thief? Or did the mysterious presence of the springs mean that this was always a place of healing and worship? We may never know, unless an archaeologist turns up evidence of a violent death. But here are a just a few mysteries and unanswered questions from Bath's earliest days. Some are mysteries because we do not know what happened, and the facts are open to different interpretations. And some are odd because they show that the nature of crime changes. Who could ever have thought that death would be meted out to monks singing in the wrong way? Or that an interest in science would have to be kept secret?

Whatever happened to Vilbia? – an unsolved mystery of Aquae Sulis

Over the years, our picture of Roman Bath, or Aquae Sulis as it should properly be called, has changed. We now know that it was much larger than was previously thought, with suburbs laid out around a well-planned, spacious, city centre. In one part of Bath, still a fashionable area, were large villas; another part of Aquae Sulis was busy with shops and craft workshops, just as it is today. Despite the strict regulations of Roman rule, there were almost certainly crimes of all types – and many remained unsolved. We know this, for when all else failed, the aggrieved victims would make a trip to the temple, and toss curses into the Sacred Spring.

These curses were addressed to the goddesses closely associated with the spring, the Celtic Sulis and the Roman goddess of wisdom, Minerva. They were scratched on lead, sometimes written backwards, although why this simple coding device was used is unclear. They were then rolled up and thrown into the waters.

The main crime seems to have been theft. Docca, for example, bemoans the loss of five denari, while Annianus, who thoughtfully provides the goddess with no less than eighteen suspects, has had six silver pieces removed from his purse. Others seem to have lost items, such as towels, jewellery, and cloaks, whilst at the baths. Should the goddess recover the items, the givers usually donated them to the goddess. Perhaps this was an indication of the fact that they did not expect to see them again. Sometimes they even donated the criminal.

'To Minerva the goddess of Sulis I have given the thief who has stolen my hooded cloak, whether slave or free, whether man or woman. He is not to buy back this gift unless with his own blood,' runs a typical complaint. However, theft was not always the problem. It is fairly easy to imagine that a full-scale family row involving a bit of double-crossing of the relatives lies behind the following outburst:

Uricalus, Docilosa his wife, Docilis his son and Docilina, Decentinus his brother, Alogiosa: the names of those who have sworn at the spring of the goddess Sulis on the 12th of April. Whosoever has perjured himself there you are to make him to pay for it to the goddess Sulis in his own blood.

But strangest of all the curses is the one which was the first to be discovered, in 1880. Even today, there is still vigorous discussion about what it means. The translation is sometimes explained as follows:

May he who carried off Vilbia from me become as liquid as the waters. [May] she who obscenely devoured her [become] dumb, whether Velvinna, Exspereus, Verianus, Severinus, Augustalis, Comitianus, Minianus, Germanilla or Jovina.

The words are scratched on to lead in the right order, although each word is reversed. This makes it extremely difficult to follow, especially as there are no gaps between the words. Worse still, the tablet is damaged, with some words missing.

In 1988 RSO Tomlin made a careful assessment of these Bath curses. Having first toned down the translation from 'she who has obscenely devoured her' simply to 'she who has stolen her,' he noted some unique features of the curse – the request to make the culprit liquid as the waters occurs nowhere else. More importantly, no other curse relates to the theft – or perhaps we should say abduction – of a woman. He therefore queried whether Vilbia was a personal name or simply a hitherto unknown word for an object. This had been done before – one suggestion had even been that Vilbia was a misreading of the word for napkin, but Tomlin dismissed this. Instead, he tentatively suggested the word was a misreading – or miswriting – of

The lead curse with the words reversed, against those who carried off Vilbia. The author

fibula, a bracelet. No record exists of another Vilbia, although there is Vellibia, which is strikingly similar. So far, so good. But his final reason for believing that Vilbia was not a person is charming but naïve. 'Common sense also suggests that the 'short list' of subjects would be shorter, and all men at that,' writes our gentle academic. Not, one has to say, necessarily. Besides the obvious assumption that Roman sexual tastes could be very eclectic, there is a more sinister answer. Could Vilbia be a child? Is this an intimation of a paedophile ring? There is yet another possibility, again assuming Vilbia to be a child. It was easy for Romans to be divorced. Is Velvinna, the first named suspect, perhaps the child's mother, whose ex-husband had kept the child against her will? Have she and a group of her friends seized Vilbia back? The anger behind the desire that the thief turns to water suggests that whoever or whatever Vilbia was, the person who wrote the curse deeply regretted the loss.

Perhaps one day another inscription will surface with the word Vilbia. We may then know whether this was indeed a person, or simply some obscure object which had been stolen. Until then, academics and visitors alike will continue to puzzle – and argue – over this unsolved mystery from the past.

The murder of Minerva – how to get rid of a goddess for good

Sulis Minerva may have ruled the springs for 300 years, but in 391 AD Christianity became the official religion. The old deities were declared pagan, the temples were destroyed and the statues of the gods and

All that we have left of the gilded statue of Minerva after her head was hacked from the body. The author

goddesses were pulled down and thrown away. In Aquae Sulis, however, Minerva had been very highly regarded, and she was, after all, not just any minor goddess but the daughter of Jupiter. Just pulling down her idol might not be enough to make her go away. And since she had been instrumental in helping the city's citizens to curse other people, it was decided that she would have to be killed off properly. The crime came to light in 1727, when some workmen, excavating a sewer in Stall Street came across a gilded head. Although some people think it may be Apollo, it is generally thought to be the head of Minerva, and is the cult statue from her temple. Microscopic examination of the head shows that it was hacked from the body – Minerva, in fact, had been murdered. The goddess had been got rid of for good.

The lady in the oven – the crime that wasn't

When the Romans left Britain, and the Saxons, Angles and Jutes swept across the country they had so long coveted, rule of law broke down in many places. Because so little is known of this period, we call it the Dark Ages. We are reliant on archaeological evidence to tell us what the troubled times were like. But the evidence is not always clear, and interpretations may change. Take the case of the lady in the oven.

In 1984–5, Bath Archaeological Trust had the opportunity to dig in Abbeygate Street, right in the heart of the old city, just south of the

Abbeygate Street today is a cheerful little street of shops in Bath's city centre – but it was here that a young woman's skull, dating from the Dark Ages, was found in an oven. Murder – or just a disturbed burial? The author

Abbey. There was much excitement when a skull was found in an oven, and even greater excitement when evidence showed that it was the severed head of young woman. The immediate assumption was that it showed, to put it in Professor Barry Cunliffe's sober words 'a decline in civilized standards of living'. It was not unreasonable to assume this. The monk Gildas, writing in the sixth century, described the Saxon invasion as a fire of vengeance, with cities destroyed, in the streets of which were 'fragments of human bodies ... with no chance of being buried save in the ruins of the houses.' This fitted precisely with the mysterious skull. Moreover, there was some evidence of local destruction. The Roman villa at Box had been destroyed by fire, and bodies had been thrown down a well at the villa at North Wraxall. In recent times, however, archaeologists have become wary of leaping to sensational conclusions, and by 2002 Peter Davenport, one of Bath's leading archaeologists, was suggesting that the head was possibly simply a disturbed medieval burial. It's another strange story to which we may never know the answer.

How did a Viking lose his sword? – another puzzle from the past

In 1980, an excavation was carried out by archaeologists along the north side of the city wall, between Upper Borough Walls and New Bond Street. The most exciting find was made by a workman when the trench was being filled in. He spotted a sword – and a rather unusual and magnificent sword it turned out to be. What surprised everyone was that it was Viking and not Saxon. It dated from about the tenth century and was made of steel which was still sharp. The steel had been given a black patina in order to show up an inscription inlaid on one side and decoration on the other. The pommel was inlaid in silver, and it was still in its fur-lined wool and steel scabbard. It clearly belonged to someone of very high status – but how did it get there? The Vikings occupied Bath in the early eleventh century, but even after a good night on the mead, the Viking's favourite tipple, it is unlikely that a Danish chief would be so careless as to drop his sword in the town ditch. Perhaps it had been kept over the centuries as an heirloom and then lost – but once again we are faced with the problem of how it came to be in the ditch outside the city wall. The only other solution is that at some stage, in some skirmish by the city wall, before the Vikings arrived in the city in force, its owner was killed and the sword fell unnoticed. It may even have been through several hands, both Saxon and Viking, in this way. So next time you stroll past the shops in New Bond Street, remember that men fought and died where today fashion and furniture jostle for our attention. Of course, you may be able to think up a better story ....

Slaughtered for singing the wrong song – how the Saxon monks of Glastonbury died for their music

It was tough being a Saxon. Hardly had the Saxons seen off or merged with the Danes, when along came the Normans, and took all the plum jobs. This included all the top appointments in the monasteries and abbeys, and many of the new men had firm ideas on how the churches should be run. It was bad enough for the Saxon monks at Bath in having John de Villula as their new bishop. He considered them boorish and uneducated, even though they had been producing beautiful, clearly written manuscripts. But for the monks at Glastonbury it was much worse. The new Abbot, Thurstan, decided he would have everybody singing in the French style, and introduced the liturgy from Fécamp. Now Glastonbury was an iconic church to the Saxons. It was associated with figures such as St Dunstan, St Patrick and Joseph of Arimathea. The Saxon monks saw no reason why they should give up years of tradition, and went on singing the old liturgy. Thurstan knew it was also act of defiance against the French masters. He was nothing if not determined. He persisted in trying to outlaw the Saxon liturgy, but without success. Despite all his threats and edicts, the Glastonbury monks kept right on singing the wrong song. Eventually, in 1083, angered by this stubborn action, he threatened them with the death penalty. He stationed archers in the nave, near the high altar, picking out those recalcitrant monks who ignored his French music. Three died and several were injured. Even William the Conqueror acknowledged you couldn't treat monks like that, and removed

Abbot Thurstan's Abbey, built in 1077, was pulled down by the next Abbot in 1100. That church was destroyed by fire in 1184, and in the rebuilding, the Lady Chapel was put on the site of the old churches. Now it too stands in ruins. Author's collection

Thurstan. However, his son, William Rufus, reinstated him, and Thurstan was still Abbot of Glastonbury on his death in 1101.

Malingering monks, a battling bishop, and a prior with a secret – a collection of less than Christian clergy

If anyone should have been setting the populace an example of good behaviour, it was surely the monks and clergy associated with Bath's principal church, the Abbey. But this was not always the case. Comments were made on several occasions that the monks' behaviour was not in accordance with the rules laid down by the Church. When Oliver King, appointed Bishop by Henry VII, came to the city he found more feasting than praying, and we are told that women were found in the precincts at inappropriate hours. When Henry VIII sent down his commissioners to assess the church during the Dissolution of the Monasteries, matters were even worse. The commissioner, Dr Layton, wrote to Thomas Cromwell that the monks were 'worse than any I have found yet in buggery and adultery, some one of them having ten women, some eight, and the rest fewer'. At least they were not at war with other monks. During the twelfth century, after John de Villula moved the seat of the bishopric from Bath to Wells, there was a power struggle between the two monasteries, with everything from political manoeuvring to open warfare. Finally they reached an agreement that it should be a double diocese, with the cathedral at Wells, but not before one bishop, Bishop Joscelin, had actually removed the name of Wells from his title altogether, signing the Magna Carta as Bishop of Bath and Glastonbury.

At least Bishop Joscelin was religious. The same could not be said of Bishop Savaric, whose activities were at best Macchiavellian and worst downright thuggish. In 1172, as a young priest, he had been fined £26 3s 4d for stealing a bow from the king's foresters. A peasant could have been executed for this, but Savaric, the cousin of the Holy Roman Emperor, got away with it. Just eight years later he was archdeacon of Northampton. Preferring fighting to preaching, he went off on the Crusades with Richard I in 1189, but was elected Bishop of Bath and Wells in 1192. He did not take up the post until a year later, being involved in negotiating Richard's release from captivity by the Emperor. Savaric played a cunning double game here, and got the king released, but only on condition that Richard wrote letters to influential people proposing that Savaric become Archbishop of Canterbury – a letter Richard smartly repudiated once he was safely back home.

When Savaric did return to England, it was the unhappy monks at Glastonbury who were in trouble again. They had never approved of the bishops of Bath and Wells having the right to interfere in their

Some dark secrets lie behind this peaceful scene in Bath's Abbey Church Yard. Oliver King's Abbey was built to improve the moral standing as well as the fabric of the church – the monks were behaving in unmonkish ways. But by the time of the Dissolution of the Monasteries, they were no better – and the Prior was indulging in strange experiments. The author

monastery, and Savaric made it clear that he intended to do just that. They appealed to the Pope, but Savaric won the case, and retaliated by beating the monks he knew had opposed him – one died. Once the monks had capitulated, Savaric decided to behave more graciously, granting money to Wells and Glastonbury, and protecting Bath from the collection for Richard's ransom. Despite all his string-pulling and bullying, however, he never rose any higher than Bishop of Bath and Wells.

Prior Gibbs is not only the last in our list – he was also the last prior of Bath. He had a dark secret which would have got him into all sorts of trouble had it been widely known. He was an alchemist. Today this is hardly a crime, but in a society dominated by church rule, this was a very dangerous secret indeed. Alchemy is not just the fore-runner of modern science – it is a philosophy, and not one that sits easily with Christianity, particularly a belief in the trinity. As late as the early eighteenth century, Isaac Newton felt impelled to keep his alchemy and his Unitarianism something known only to a few, for some of his acquaintances had been imprisoned for their beliefs. We know about Gibbs (or Holloway as he also called himself) thanks to the inquisitive Elias Ashmole, who could never resist a good story. He wrote about a mysterious tincture found in a wall at Bath Abbey, belonging to the last Prior of Bath Abbey, who had received it through an intermediary from George Ripley. Prior Gibbs had hidden it in a wall of the Abbey during the time it was suppressed, but on returning a few days later could not find it again. This Prior passed on his secret to Thomas Charnock, another alchemist. Ashmole takes up the story in his own words:

> *Shortly after the dissolution of Bath Abbey, upon the pulling down some of the walls, there was a glass found in a wall full of Red Tincture, which being flung away to a dunghill, forthwith it coloured it, exceeding red. This dunghill (or rubbish) was after fetched away by boat by Bathwick men, and laid in Bathwick field, and in the places where it was spread, for a long time after, the corn grew wonderfully rank, thick and high: insomuch as it was there looked upon as a wonder. This Belcher and Foster (2 shoemakers of Bath, who died about 20 years since) can very well remember; as also one called Old Anthony, a butcher who died about 12 years since.*
>
> *This relation I recd: from Mr. Rich: Wakeman Town Clerk of Bath; (who hath often heard the said Old Anthony tell this story) in Michaelmas Term 1651.*

Gibbs was so distraught at having lost this tincture that, according to Charnock, 'he did go blind and mad in himself, and for the rest of his days did wander diverse ways about the country, led by a boy'. And with that rather sad end, we leave this litany of mysteries and secrets, and turn to more serious crime.

CHAPTER 2

Ramblers and Gamblers

Some of eighteenth-century Bath's less desirable visitors – fortune hunters, gamblers and highwaymen

As Bath became fashionable in the early eighteenth century, after the visits of Queen Anne, there followed in the wake of society visitors a rag, tag and bobtail crew of shadier characters, all anxious to relieve gullible tourists of their money. No wonder that Bath's most famous Master of Ceremonies, Richard Beau Nash, laid down a series of rules for society to follow and did his best to protect the unwary from the traps which were laid for them.

Leading the way, and often appearing respectable, were the fortune hunters. As Bath became the place where the nobility gathered for pleasure, it also became a place to display unmarried daughters on the marriage market, in the hope of making a good catch. Unfortunately, among the shoals of suitable suitors were some sharks, ready to woo an heiress and elope with her. With no married woman's property act, their fortune became their husband's on marriage. Nash, if he got word of such a misalliance, would often try to stop it, but he had to be careful not to alert the gossips to the situation. If once a girl's reputation was tarnished, her chances of marriage were gone. On one occasion, a lady entered one of the assembly rooms with her younger daughter, the elder having opted to stay at home. Nash walked up to the lady and said, 'Madam, you had better be at home.' Offended, she turned away, only for Nash to follow her and repeat the words more earnestly. She suddenly realized that something was amiss and hurried home – just in time to prevent her elder daughter from eloping with a fortune hunter.

Once in a while such an elopement ended happily. The fortune hunter, once he had his hands on the money, sometimes discovered respectability, and became an outspoken critic of such immoral proceedings. But this was the exception. All too often the outcome was disgrace and poverty for the girl. Fanny Braddock was such a one. Arriving in Bath at the age of nineteen, with a fortune of £10,000 – equal to £1,000,000 today – she considered the income from this

Richard 'Beau' Nash, Bath's most famous Master of Ceremonies and a gambler himself, often stepped in to dissuade the young from gambling or to prevent an unwise elopement. Author's collection

insufficient for her life-style and turned to gambling. In the meantime, she turned down many suitors, some attracted by her beauty and some by her fortune. Inevitably, she fell for a fortune hunter. Beau Nash warned her against him, but to no avail. When he was arrested for debt, she traced him and paid his debts. For a while he disappeared, but reappeared when he was need of more money. Despite running through Fanny's rapidly dwindling funds, he was arrested, and later died in gaol. By now, Fanny, with little money and no reputation, was shunned by her family and friends. She was 'rescued'

Bath's social atmosphere, where men and women could meet easily in the Baths – as bathers or spectators – and the Pump Room, made it easy for fortune-hunters to meet unsuspecting girls. Author's collection

In Nash's day the two sets of Assembly Rooms were in the centre of town. Both sets can be seen in this picture – those in the foreground survived to become known as the Lower Rooms, but burnt down in 1820. Dame Lindsey's Rooms are in the background, with the three large circular windows. They were demolished in the 1790s, but had long ceased to be Assembly Rooms. Author's collection

by Dame Lindsey, who ran one of the Assembly Rooms in Bath and employed her to lure punters to the gaming tables.

Nash stepped in again and persuaded the architect John Wood to take Fanny, whom Wood called Sylvia, as a nanny. Reluctantly she went, but while in Wood's house she seems to have developed a very close relationship with him – quite how close is open to speculation. Nevertheless, she was by now very depressed. One night, while Wood was away from home, she took her girdle and hanged herself. Her brother, on hearing of her suicide, remarked unsympathetically, 'Poor Fanny! I always thought she would play till she would be forced to tuck herself up.'

Despite the scandal resulting from this death, the fortune hunters did not go away. All the time Bath was a marriage market, they circled hopefully. As late as 1785, a young Scottish heiress called Catherine Gordon of Gight fell for the charms of the widowed Captain John Byron. He was, indeed, extremely charming. His first wife had been the wife of the Marquis of Leeds until John Byron had persuaded her to elope with him. After the divorce he married her, and one child was born, Augusta. Augusta's mother died in 1784, and a year later John was on the hunt for funds. Catherine Gordon was prepared to supply them. They were married in May 1785 and it took just two years for Byron to run through most of the fortune. He fled to France to escape

Catherine Gordon of Gight was ensnared by the fortune-hunting Captain John Byron. Author's collection

his creditors, where Catherine joined him. Augusta was soon to have a half-brother, born in 1788, and christened George Gordon. He is better known to us as the poet, Lord Byron. The family was constantly on the move, dodging debt collectors, although Catherine managed to retrieve part of her inheritance from the creditors. It was invested in a way which prevented her husband from getting his hands on it, and provided Catherine with an annual income of £150. By now she and her husband were living apart, although their relations were amicable, and he often visited her. But once again he was forced to flee to France – and to retreat to revolution-torn France in 1790 shows a certain desperation. He died there in 1791, having run through the fortunes of two women.

Fortune hunting, if of dubious morality, was not actually a crime. Gambling, even before the Government decided to control it, tottered uneasily between legality and something much shadier. With the aristocracy prepared to play high – that is, for large sums of money – it was inevitable that the criminal element would be attracted. Card sharps were endemic at Bath's gaming tables, although they often met violent punishment when detected. One was thrown out of a first floor

Nash received letters from friends and acquaintances about gambling, and some were published after his death in Goldsmith's Life of Nash. *This one is deploring the way the young and inexperienced get inveigled into gaming.* The author

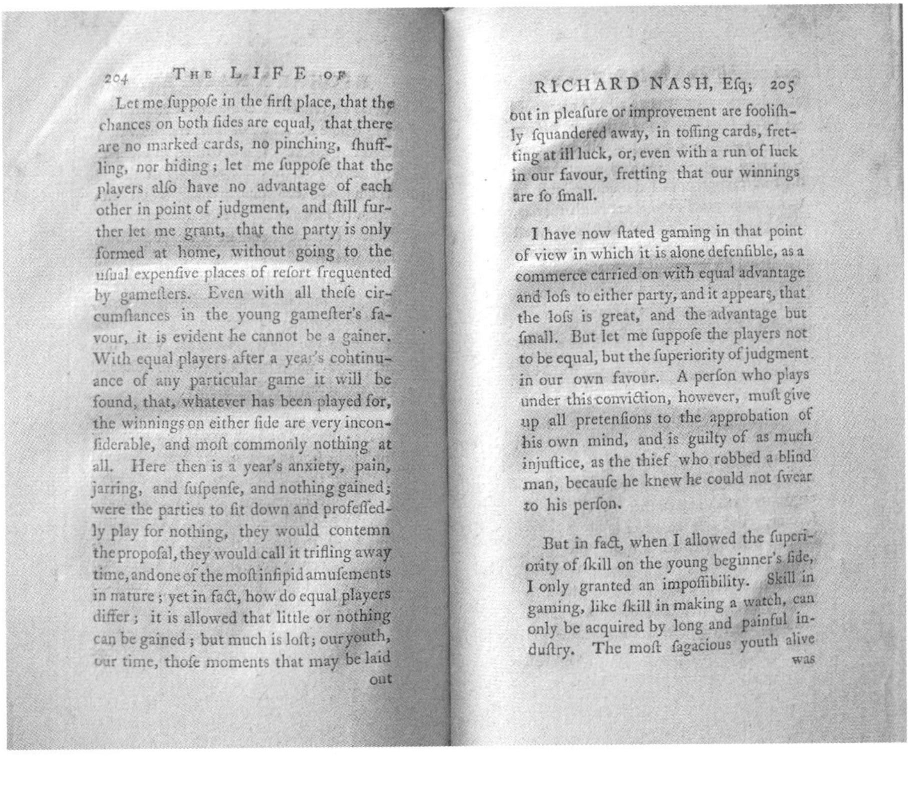

204 THE LIFE OF

Let me ſuppoſe in the firſt place, that the chances on both ſides are equal, that there are no marked cards, no pinching, ſhuffling, nor hiding; let me ſuppoſe that the players alſo have no advantage of each other in point of judgment, and ſtill further let me grant, that the party is only formed at home, without going to the uſual expenſive places of reſort frequented by gameſters. Even with all theſe circumſtances in the young gameſter's favour, it is evident he cannot be a gainer. With equal players after a year's continuance of any particular game it will be found, that, whatever has been played for, the winnings on either ſide are very inconſiderable, and moſt commonly nothing at all. Here then is a year's anxiety, pain, jarring, and ſuſpenſe, and nothing gained; were the parties to ſit down and profeſſedly play for nothing, they would contemn the propoſal, they would call it trifling away time, and one of the moſt inſipid amuſements in nature; yet in fact, how do equal players differ; it is allowed that little or nothing can be gained; but much is loſt; our youth, our time, thoſe moments that may be laid out

RICHARD NASH, Eſq; 205

out in pleaſure or improvement are fooliſhly ſquandered away, in toſſing cards, fretting at ill luck, or, even with a run of luck in our favour, fretting that our winnings are ſo ſmall.

I have now ſtated gaming in that point of view in which it is alone defenſible, as a commerce carried on with equal advantage and loſs to either party, and it appears, that the loſs is great, and the advantage but ſmall. But let me ſuppoſe the players not to be equal, but the ſuperiority of judgment in our own favour. A perſon who plays under this conviction, however, muſt give up all pretenſions to the approbation of his own mind, and is guilty of as much injuſtice, as the thief who robbed a blind man, becauſe he knew he could not ſwear to his perſon.

But in fact, when I allowed the ſuperiority of ſkill on the young beginner's ſide, I only granted an impoſſibility. Skill in gaming, like ſkill in making a watch, can only be acquired by long and painful induſtry. The moſt ſagacious youth alive was window. When complaining of his treatment to a wit called Samuel Foote, he asked Foote what he should do. 'Do?' replied Foote. 'Why it is a plain case. Never play so high again as long as you live!' Another, Mr Newman, was suspected by another player of palming cards. Without further ado, his opponent picked up a fork and pinned his hand to the table, with the comment: 'Sir, if you have not a card hidden under that hand, I apologise.' History does not relate if he was correct in his surmise. Once strict rules came in to stop vast sums changing hands at the tables, even the operators frequently found themselves in the courts.

It was this passion for high play – or playing deep, as it was also known – that caused the Government to sit up and take notice. Beau Nash, who was very conscious that if Bath gained a reputation for being the ruin of young people, society might stop coming, is reputed to have stepped in on several occasions to persuade young people not to get caught up in it. One favourite trap was to encourage beginners by letting them win – hence beginner's luck – but once they were confident and started placing higher bets, the cards mysteriously turned against them. Dice were fixed, dice boxes were rigged, cards were marked, often by pricking tiny holes so that those in the know could tell which cards were being dealt, or by inserting tiny needles so far into certain cards that only those in the know could tell they were there. Not everyone disapproved of the cardsharps. Lord Chesterfield said he preferred to play against them, for when he won, they paid up, whereas if he won against gentlemen, 'they frequently behaved so genteelly I get nothing but words and polite apologies for my money'.

Nash, for all his concern about the unwary being trapped by such tricks, still continued to earn his living at the tables. Suddenly the Government, in an effort to stamp out excesses at the gaming tables handed him a windfall. They brought in a rule which banned games with numbers on. The variety of games was such that every time they brought in an act the gamesters found a way around it. Besides cards, there were dice games such as hazard, and a wide assortment played on what were called the tables, of which backgammon was just one. Most, except, for some reason, backgammon, had been outlawed, only for the government to see them replaced with others such as 'Roly Poly', or Roulette, which had no cards or dice or tables. But, by banning games with numbers, they thought they had solved the problem. They had not, however, banned letters. An enterprising gamester called Cook replaced the numbers on the roulette wheel with the letters E and O, standing for even and odd. However, simply betting on two letters gave the punter an even chance and the rule of gaming tables is 'never give a sucker an even break'. To swing the odds in the bank's favour, some pockets had a bar painted on them. If

Lord Chesterfield said he preferred to play against professional gamblers – they paid their debts. Author's collection

the ball went into a barred E, the Os lost as normal, but the Es won nothing. Their stake had to stay on the table for the next time round. That simple device swung the odds dramatically in favour of the bank.

This game was first introduced at Tunbridge Wells, where Nash was Master of Ceremonies in the summer, never a fashionable time in Bath. After some behind-the-scenes dealing with promoters of the game, Nash ended up with a percentage of the profits. Keen to

Winners and losers – mainly losers by the look on their faces – at an EO table. This cartoon is entitled 'The Fashionable Vowels.' Author's collection

augment his income, he introduced the game to the rooms at Bath, taking a slightly smaller percentage. Convinced that it was legal, the gamesters, punters and promoters took to EO with enthusiasm. Charles Burney reported seeing 1,000 guineas in a heap on an EO table at Bath. But the government had also been taking legal advice and they were assured that EO was covered by the Gaming Act. They ordered councils to crack down, but in Bath, nervous at offending some of the influential people to be found at the tables, the authorities vacillated. It was not until 1750 that determined action was taken. On 8 January 1750 the paper reported:

> *Last Tuesday night Charles Stone Esq, Mayor of this City, accompanied by several of the Corporation, and attended by proper officers, went to a house by Westgate, kept by one R Richards, for they had information that an EO table was there. When they arrived, they went upstairs to where the table was, and found about 16 persons playing; the gamesters, on seeing the magistrates, were put into great confusion and immediately extinguished all the candles; two of them jumped out of the window, and made their escape, tho' one of them fell into the Airy* [*the space in front of the basement windows*], *and was like to have been killed. The magistrates prevented the escape of the others, procured some lights, took down their names, and sent them, two at a time, to prison.*

> *They afterwards pulled down the table, carried it onto the street, procured some faggots, and burnt it amidst a great number of spectators, who were very merry on the occasion.*

Yet still the gamblers persisted. For the rich and powerful, such as Lord Chesterfield, there would always be places where play for high stakes could be found. As late as 1787, the paper reported the arrest of two men, John Twycross and Richard Watendell of Alfred St, for running a Faro Table. They were fined £1,800, of which two thirds went to the hospital and one third to the informer. Alfred Street, it should be added, is in a highly respectable and fashionable part of the city, right beside the Upper Assembly Rooms. Some people, it seems, would never learn.

Card sharps were on the fringes of respectable society, tolerated by cynical and pragmatic gamblers such as Lord Chesterfield and the Duchess of Marlborough. Out in the darkness, however, lurked the lawless, also drawn to Bath by the rich pickings offered by tourists. Lowest of the low were the footpads, known in modern times as muggers. In December 1751, 'about ten o'clock, Mr Philip Brown, Nursery Man, was attacked near the end of the Terrace Walk in Kingsmead by two footpads, one of whom presented a pistol to his

Views such of this one of Bath in the 1740s were entitled prospects, but to the card-sharps, pickpockets and footpads, Bath offered the prospect of wealth. Meanwhile many a highwayman must have gazed down on Bath, admiring not the view but the arrival of rich pickings. Author's collection

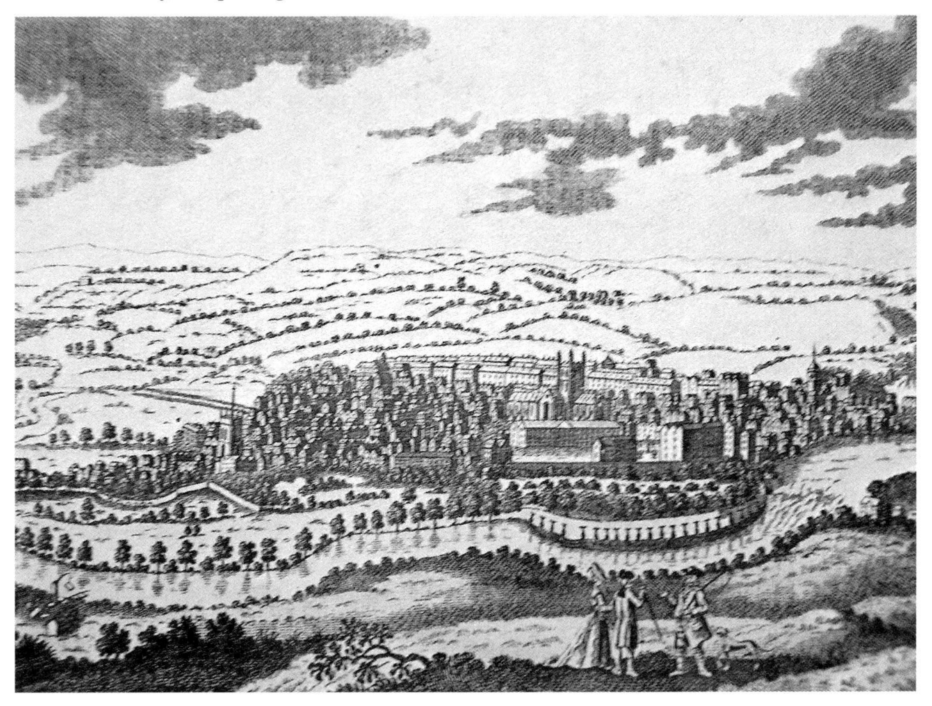

breast, and bid him stand; upon which he catched hold of the pistol and wrenched it from the fellow's hand; and then they made off. The pistol was loaded with a ball and coarse cannon powder; it has a screw barrel and on it is engraved J Jenkins.' Such stories were common fare in the papers of the time. If the footpads were the lowest of the low then there was one group who considered themselves the cream of the criminal classes. They were the highwaymen.

From the moment travellers set out from their inns in London, they were at risk. Travelling to Bath, they had to cross Hounslow Heath, a notorious haunt of highwaymen, despite the rows of gibbets with their gruesome cargo: the rotting bodies of hanged robbers, intended to deter would-be criminals. A number of busy roads went across the bleak heath, where the only industry was gunpowder production, and where even the sheep were so poor and thin they were described as 'greyhound-like'. The road between Kensington and Knightsbridge was no safer, and if the traveller escaped the London highwaymen, the Bath neighbourhood had some of its own. In 1745, the Bath Journal carried the following rather florid advertisement:

> This is to inform the Publick, That the NEW ROAD leading from BECKHAMPTON near MARLBOROUGH in WILTSHIRE (through CALNE and CHIPPENHAM, Two pleasant Market Towns) to PICKWICK, in the same County, is now compleatly finished, whereby Persons travelling from LONDON, to BATH and BRISTOL, may avoid BOWDEN and BAGDON HILLS, too well known and dreaded by Travellers to need to be described here. This is also the nearest and the Post Road, and during the Summer Season will be render'd more pleasant, by the Use of Stanley and Studley Commons, by which the Length of Way will be very considerably shortened, and COACHES. &c, may keep the Turf for four or five Miles together. On this Road also are most convenient watering Places every Two or Three Miles throughout the Whole, ADVANTAGES which it is well known the SANDY LANE ROAD has not.
> ☞ N.B. GENTLEMEN travelling the Two Roads, either in Carriages or on Horse-back, are desired to mark the Difference from their Watches, in point of TIME.

The reason the two hills mentioned were so notorious was that, firstly, they were very steep, and extra horses had to be used to drag coaches to the top, especially on Bagdon Hill (usually known as Beacon Hill). Going up or coming down, progress was slow, which made it much easier for the highwaymen to stop the coaches. At the top of Beacon Hill there was a rather bleak common where robberies frequently took place. Sandy Lane was a small sanctuary on this dangerous stretch,

Beacon Hill from Sandy Lane – for travellers to Bath, the steep descent of Bowden Hill came shortly afterwards, while for those who had come the other way, this was the daunting sight that faced them after the climb from Lacock. The author

This muddy, treacherous lane was the Old Bath Road as it descended Beacon Hill – it probably looked even worse than it does now, and coaches had to go slowly. The author

although those travelling to Bath would see the welcome sight of the inns at Lacock when they finally reached the bottom of Bowden Hill. It was not unknown for Beau Nash to ride out to Sandy Lane to greet noble visitors, for his presence was enough to deter the gentlemen of the road. Perturbed by the fact that such villains might deter visitors coming to Bath, he employed agents to try to catch any robbers who operated close to the city, sometimes using entrapment to do so.

Despite this, the thefts continued. In December 1746, the Bath Journal reported that the Bristol stage was held up by two highwaymen who robbed the passengers of £17 in money and a silver hilted sword. They overtook the coach and one proceeded to bring the horses to a stop while the other performed the robbery. In April the following year, Mr Gardener, an ironmonger of Stroud, was attacked on his way to Bristol at Petty France, 'by a single highwayman mounted on a black Gelding who robb'd him of his Watch and about thirty Pounds in Money and made off'. This thief performed the favourite highwayman's trick of cutting the girths of the saddle to prevent pursuit, but did it so violently that he fatally wounded the horse.

One notorious and particularly ruffianly thief was John Poulter, also known as Baxter. He had his home in, of all things, an old chapel, at a place called Chapel Plaister, near Box on the Bath to London Road. Built for the use of pilgrims on the way to Glastonbury, part of the chapel had become a small cottage, while the other part was an ale-house. Poulter was eventually caught and hanged, and while in gaol confessed that he had murdered his one-time master, Dr Shakerley, Archdeacon of Wells, for the money he knew was kept in the house. Having shot him, he had so arranged the body that the coroner's jury decided it was suicide. During his trial, the landlady of the ale-house gave evidence. Asked if she had not been frightened by the sight of his pistols, she laughed and said that they were by no means the only pistols she had seen loaded in that kitchen.

Sundays were the highwayman's day of rest, since people were not supposed to travel on the Lord's Day (and if they did, the turnpike trusts charged them double). The numbers of highwaymen began to decline after about 1750, although the incidence of robbery was still frighteningly high. Even in the nineteenth century they were still around, although operating in gangs. As late as June 1835, the *Bath Chronicle* regretted having to report that 'Mr Joseph Pegler of Corsham was robbed near Box of £49 by 5 ruffians who on his making a courageous resistance, ill-treated him in the most savage and barbarous manner.' It explains why the public took so enthusiastically to the railway.

This old chapel was home to John Poulter aka John Baxter. The author

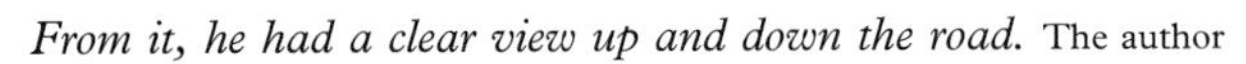

From it, he had a clear view up and down the road. The author

Palmer's Mail Coach gave speed and security to mail and travellers. Author's collection

One innovation that helped to reduce the numbers of highwaymen was the introduction of the mail coach, in 1784. Hitherto, postboys rode with the mail on horse-back, a method which was open at best to accident and at worst to corruption. The postboys, who were unarmed, were often robbed, and were sometimes suspected of being accomplices while pretending to be victims. To try to avoid loss of money, people sending bills of exchange through the post would cut them in half, sending one half by one post, the other by the next. The highwaymen got wise to this, and would lay in wait for the second post. The cost of employing postboys had to be borne by those sending letters, and John Palmer of Bath saw that if coaches were travelling the same route, they could easily carry the mail. If the very latest technology was used to produce a coach that could travel faster, with a series of reliable inns providing fresh horses to keep the coach on the move, it would be harder to stop them. He also proposed employing of an armed guard on each coach to deter robbery.

The weapon used was a blunderbuss, which fired a large quantity of shot through a trumpet-shaped barrel, thereby inflicting considerable damage without the need for accurate aiming. It certainly deterred highwaymen but also introduced a new hazard to country life. 'These guards shoot at dogs, hogs, sheep and poultry as they pass the road and even in towns, to the great terror and danger of the inhabitants,' wrote one indignant observer. One guard, during a quarrel at a turnpike, shot and killed the gate-keeper. They were not averse to a bit of poaching, or at least aiding those who were involved in it. Another guard, on the Southampton mail, was suspected of smuggling, but refused to allow the Customs to search the mail for evidence. The Post Office supported him, saying that no one had a right to carry out such a search; the guard was, however, warned about his conduct.

Modern life may present its problems, but the ramblers and gamblers who made Bath such a trap for the innocent and unwary have long gone.

CHAPTER 3

'The child was born dead'

The sad story of infanticide in the City of Bath

Anyone studying the coroners' reports of Bath in the eighteenth and nineteenth centuries could be forgiven for thinking that Bath was a city of dead babies. At times it seems one could hardly step out of doors without tripping over them. One witness, in 1778, was collecting worms at night to go fishing, a candle in his hand, when he found one. Early one morning in 1791 a labourer called John Gane had already had a bad start to his morning when he had to catch one of the horses in his care which had broken out of a field before heading for the brass mills at Twerton. On his way past Spring Gardens, a pleasure garden on the east bank of the River Avon, his dog found a dead baby.

Frequently the babies were found in open spaces such as the Ham, ground on the south side of the city, but often these sad little corpses were discovered in a privy at the bottom of the garden. One was found in the communal privy at the back of Cornwell Row, in Walcot Street. The baby was wrapped in a blue and white handkerchief and covered in filth. Despite this, the kindly people of Cornwell Row rescued it, and Sarah Savage took the tiny body and washed it, ready for burial. Not that the up-market parts of Bath were any freer of dead babies. One was found in the privy of Mr Duffield's house in Milsom Street, a library and bookshop frequented by the best in society. Another was found in the privy of a house in The Circus, in very curious circumstances. One dark evening, a housemaid, on her way to visit the necessary house, as the privy was sometimes known, was startled by something – she knew not what. A footman came with her and they saw a large black cat run into the privy. When the footman chased it, it jumped down into the trench beneath. As the footman went to pull it out he found a baby with its throat cut. All the female servants were questioned, but no one knew anything.

This was unusual, if the baby had indeed been born to a servant. All too often they were only too ready to give witness against the unhappy mother. Despite this, very few mothers were ever charged with infanticide. The verdict was nearly always that the baby had been

Even in the gracious surroundings of the Circus, a dead baby was found in a privy. The author

born dead, or had died immediately afterwards. Here are two tragic tales, from very different parts of Bath.

Brock Street – the baby in the trunk, 4 January 1814

Mr Durell, of No. 30 Brock Street, between The Circus and the Royal Crescent, must have found his domestic arrangements severely disrupted when two of his servants were involved in an inquest on a dead baby. His cook, Ann Ashley, had complained of feeling sick on the

Mr Durell's house at No. 30 Brock Street is now occupied by an eminent company of ecologists and landscape architects. The author

previous evening and went upstairs several times, once for half an hour. At 10.00 pm she complained of feeling cold, had some gruel and went to bed, as did her fellow servant Elizabeth Young, who slept in the same room.

Early the next morning, Elizabeth got up at 5.45 am and left Ann in bed. An hour later, she had still not appeared, so Elizabeth, who was probably getting quite exasperated by not having someone to help her with the chores, went back upstairs to find out where Ann was. She was still in bed, so Elizabeth asked her to get up and help with the washing. She eventually appeared at 7.30 am. A quarter of an hour later, Elizabeth went back up to their room, and discovered Ann's trunk closed and locked, which, she said, was unusual. It has to be said that the image of Elizabeth Young that starts to emerge is of someone who was incurably nosy, especially when she admits she had a key to Ann's trunk. Curiosity, she said, induced her to take a look inside. She was about to get an unpleasant shock, for inside was a dead baby in a close stool pan. A close stool was what today we would call a commode. There was blood about the baby's head.

Mrs Durell was promptly informed, and she called a surgeon, Mr King. She also sent Ann Ashley to bed, having, it appears, rather kinder feelings than her heartless, nosy servant. Mrs Durell stated she had no idea that her cook was with child, and never saw her making any baby clothes.

Ann Ashley and Elizabeth Young would doubtless have slept in the garret, whose windows are just visible above the parapet. The author

Ann at first denied that the baby was born alive, but Mr King called in another surgeon, Clement Cruttwell, who said the lungs were fully inflated and the child was fully grown. At this Ann changed her story. She had, she said, felt labour pains coming on the previous evening, so she sat on a close stool. The baby then fell in, giving a single cry. Not having a light, she went downstairs and on her return she found the child dead. Incredibly, the jury accepted this evidence and declared that the male child had 'accidentally, casually and by misfortune, died'. Mr Durell's cook must have been extremely relieved.

Avon Street – the baby who sighed twice, 1 January 1820

Our second story comes from Avon Street. Here, with its brothels, stables, pubs and lodgings for the poor, there must have been many illegitimate children – and many babies who saw the light but briefly before being despatched. Yet that does not mean that the street's inhabitants were indifferent to these events, or that these reluctant mothers were not distressed by their clandestine births, as this next story shows.

The first witness at the inquest was Elizabeth Ody of No. 45 Avon Street. She said that at 10.00 am she had been going towards the wash house at the back of her house when she saw marks of blood on the

Even in the late nineteenth century, Avon Street was still a poor area of Bath, but was a tight-knit community. Museum of Bath at Work

snow in the courtyard. Seeing a fellow lodger, Ann Highman, a single woman, coming in at the street door she asked her how this had come about. Ann replied that her cousin had 'broke something in his inside' and the blood had come from thence and from his nose, and that she had fallen down with the utensil into which it was put and had spilt it. Elizabeth Ody was clearly dubious about this, for she mentioned it to another lodger, Maria Dawson. They went to the water closet, where they found the afterbirth of a child. The two then called a constable who went to Ann Highman's room, where she was lying with a dead baby.

Maria Dawson, who was married, said that about a fortnight before she had slept with Ann Highman. Why she had done this instead of sleeping with her husband we are not told. She suspected that Ann was with child and said so, but Ann denied it. After the discovery of the afterbirth, Ann was still denying she had given birth, but then said that she been delivered of a child. She had 'been to the Privy in the morning when she was suddenly taken ill and then delivered of the child before she could call for assistance'. She told another witness it was all over in the course of half an hour. 'The child had sighed twice and died.'

There is something very moving about this little detail – this little tragedy enacted by Ann Highman, alone in the snowy courtyard of an Avon Street lodging house. And she had not left the baby in a filthy privy or thrown it into the river nearby. When discovered by the constable and Mrs Dawson, the baby was lying on a box in Ann's room, with a cloth laid over it, as though ready for burial. She had certainly intended to keep it, for she had even prepared baby linen. As with the sorry story of the baby in the privy at Cornwell Row, it seems there was more tenderness in Bath's poorer areas than among the frightened servants of the upper town, desperate to keep their jobs at all costs. In the surgeon's view, the baby would not have survived. Having examined the lungs, he felt sure that it would never have breathed properly, and probably died during the birth. Once again the mother was cleared, this time with much greater justification.

In an age when justice was often draconian, why did so many inquest juries take such a lenient attitude to what to us seems like a dreadful crime? Only in the rarest cases, when the child had obvious signs of violence, was the mother charged. Even then it was difficult to get a conviction, for juries were reluctant to condemn a woman who had been through so much anguish to hanging or transportation. There were a number of reasons for this apparent humanitarianism. First of all, many took the view that the unhappy woman had been punished enough. She had endured months of anxiety, hiding her condition from others while feeling all the uncomfortable effects of

This old outdoor privy has survived as a garden feature at Upper Shockerwick, near Bath. The author

At Banwell, this nineteenth century privy has been restored. This is how the privies in the Circus and Avon Street might have appeared, although the communal one in Cornwell Row was probably a row of such seats. The author

pregnancy. She then had all the distress and guilt which would, in many cases, never leave her. We certainly should not blame these women – in our day, science has made it easy to avoid an unwanted pregnancy. In those days, there were no contraceptives for women, while those for men were expensive, unreliable, and unpleasant. So the only way out was an abortion, with all the attendant risks – or to wait and kill the child at birth. Many a juryman at many an inquest must have known that his wife or lover had taken a similar route to the pathetic parent before them. But there were pragmatic reasons as well. If the woman had not killed her baby, then she would almost certainly had to turn to parish relief to keep it. Few would employ a servant with an illegitimate child in tow. Infanticide saved the authorities money. Ann Ashley was probably later dismissed (although perhaps with the tender-hearted Mrs Durell as her mistress she was spared that) but at least she would have found work elsewhere, especially if she was a good cook. Furthermore, if the baby was born to a servant in a wealthy household and there was a trial, not only would the family be subjected to the scandal, but awkward questions might be raised as to who was the father.

It was so much easier for everyone if the verdict was that 'the child was born dead'.

CHAPTER 4

The Mob on the March

Some stories of what happened when the mob went on the streets

Bath was not always the safe, prosperous environment promoted by the guidebooks or portrayed in novels and prints. The prints deliberately show well-dressed fashionable people in the streets – the artists wanted people to come to Bath and buy their pictures as souvenirs. Only satirical cartoonists like Gillray and Rowlandson dared to show a seamier side of life, and even then their work was aimed at those who could afford to pay for it. As we have seen in an earlier chapter, the city attracted a motley crowd of scroungers, gamblers, thieves, and con men all anxious to prey on the hapless visitor. And then there were those who had started by working industriously but had fallen on hard times and ended up begging on the streets or, in the case of many young girls, selling their bodies to stay alive. Jane Austen does not mention them simply because they were not noteworthy – they were part of the everyday scene. The apparently affluent city had a dark underbelly about which the guidebooks were silent. Throughout the eighteenth and nineteenth centuries, too, there was political unrest, often caused by those who saw the injustice of the enormous gap between rich and poor, and demanded the right to put their view. Tom Paine, in *The Rights of Man*, used the city as an example of a place where human rights were denied. 'In a city, such for instance as Bath,' he wrote, 'which contains between twenty and thirty thousand inhabitants, the right of electing representatives to Parliament is monopolised by about thirty-one persons.' The councillors not only chose the candidates, they also elected them. The disaffected, the poor, those with nothing to lose, were only too ready to go on the streets to support anyone who stood up against what they perceived as uncaring authority. Occasionally, the views they supported were those of unscrupulous rabble-rousers; sometimes they simply took over what started out as well-meaning demonstrations. The results were nearly always terrifying, and sometimes fatal.

One cause of irritation was turnpike roads. Nearly every road user opposed the introduction of these (with the notable exception of

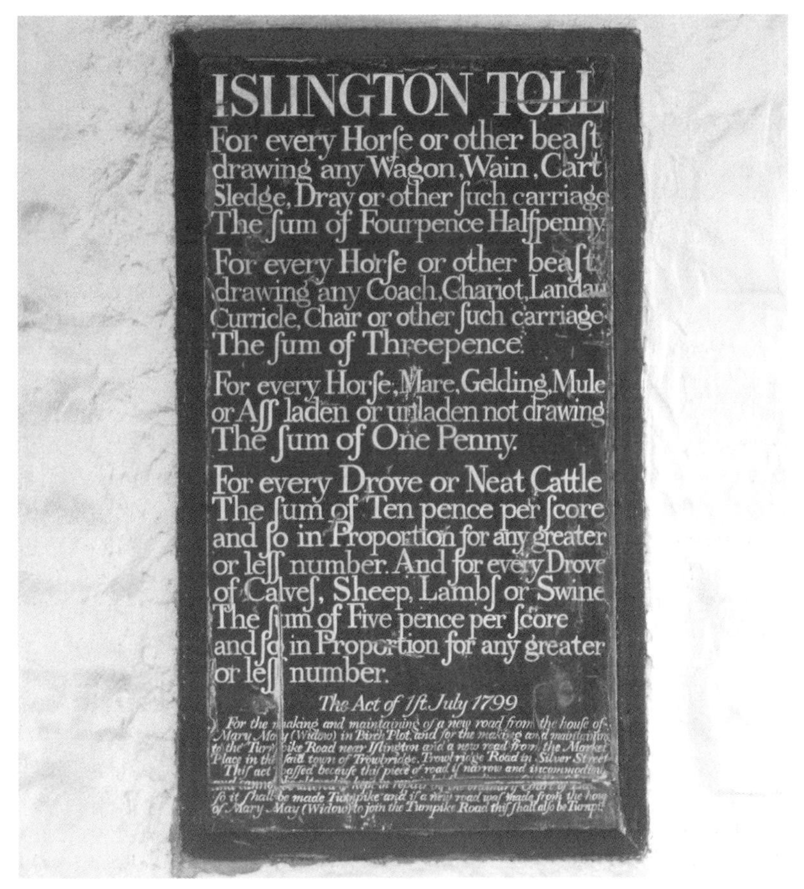

The charges on turnpike roads were a continuing source of irritation. As this one at Trowbridge shows, it was not cheap to travel on them. In modern times 1 penny is now worth about 25p. Driving a herd of twenty cattle past this turnpike would have cost you the equivalent of £5. Andrew Swift

Daniel Defoe, who had the sense to see that the only way to improve the terrible road conditions was by getting people to pay for them). In 1727, the colliers in the Bristol area objected to paying tolls on their coal, so they took the simple if drastic measure of pulling down four tollgates. When they found the one at Totterdown, on the Bath road, had been re-erected, they demolished it again and swore they would bring no coal into the city nor allow any turnpikes on their roads until they were exempted from the tolls. When four of the demonstrators were arrested, the mob gathered outside the gaol and threatened to demolish that as well.

In 1749, a large crowd combined a pub crawl with pulling down turnpikes. The *Bath Journal* reported that they had 'destroyed the turnpike house at Toghill, about four miles from this city and burnt all the timber belonging. They then went to the public house at Toghill and drank a great deal of liquor; afterwards to the public houses on Lansdown, from thence to Bitton, and crossed the river at Keynsham, where they continued and, at Busselton, all that night; and have been almost ever since, wandering about the country raising contributions.'

The colliers also destroyed the lock at Saltford on the River Avon, after it had been made navigable. They were concerned about Shropshire coal being imported into the city. They left two threatening letters, which stated that 'this attempt was made by only 300 men, as the beginning of much greater mischief that was intended against the navigation by as many thousand, unless an immediate stop was put to the sending of any more coals by water.' It was all in vain. The lock was repaired, and the government brought in the death penalty for anyone found damaging a waterway.

West Country weavers and spinners also took to the streets when things were bad. In 1622, English cloth was out of favour, partly due to a disastrous intervention in the trade by the government. The High Sheriff of Somerset wrote that: 'the multitudes of poor spinners, weavers, etc., in the county, now without work, tend to mutiny.' Weavers were particularly vociferous. Their craft was labour intensive and subject to fluctuations in the market. As the work was somewhat dusty, weavers were famous for their ability to drink. They were also united in their determination to defend their skilled trade and were often better educated than other workers. All this meant they were a formidable and organised group. The government therefore brought in a law, in 1726, which forbad textile workers from joining clubs whose aims were the improvement of conditions, pay and hours. Employers, however, were at liberty to form committees and cartels to keep the workforce in its place. If the government thought the threat of imprisonment and hard labour would deter the west country weavers, they were wrong. In May 1726, textile workers marched into Trowbridge, armed with clubs, wearing high hats and with their faces 'smooted' (blacked). They broke into the workshops of some of the masters who were paying low wages, cut cloth from the looms, shredded it into tiny pieces and left, 'without being known or molested'. A similar protest in Bristol, in August that year, however, left many weavers injured, having been shot – 'but not fatally', according to the local newspaper. In December, the weavers of Melksham and Bradford broke into the homes of some master weavers and clothiers, smashing looms.

The trouble subsided on that occasion thanks to the one man in authority who realised that the weavers might have a case. His name was John Cooper, and he was a Trowbridge magistrate. He stepped in after another riot, caused by sending some weavers to gaol, had ended with one man dead and two wounded at the hands of soldiers stationed in the town. Cooper persuaded the Bradford-on-Avon magistrate (and clothier) Thomas Methuen that his actions had been over-harsh, and that he had been influenced by clothiers who were treating their workers badly. After he dispatched a report to the government in London, an investigator was sent down. He talked to many of the craftsmen involved, and found that they were being subjected to sharp practices by their masters. It then appears pressure was brought to bear on these masters by more enlightened, or perhaps simply more frightened, employers, so that for a time the matter seemed resolved.

But unrest continued to simmer, especially when machines were brought in to replace skilled workers. The most hated of these machines was the scribbling horse, a frame which could scribble (or card) the wool, ready for spinning. In 1791, trouble erupted in the heart of Bradford on Avon. Today there is a small park down by the river overlooked by a rather grand, early eighteenth century mansion called Westbury House. It is hard to imagine the violent scenes that took place here on the evening of 14 May 1791. At the end of that dreadful evening, hardly a window in the building was left intact, and much of the furniture in the house had been destroyed. Outside three people lay dead, with many others wounded. The house had always

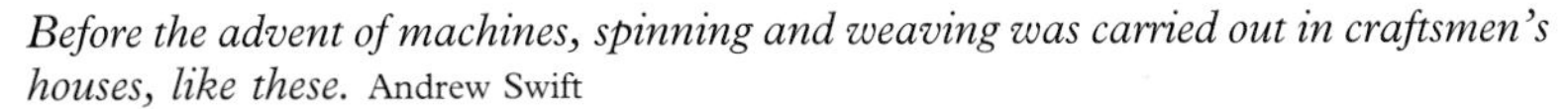

Before the advent of machines, spinning and weaving was carried out in craftsmen's houses, like these. Andrew Swift

Bradford on Avon, with its weavers' cottages and the later large mills. Andrew Swift

belonged to clothiers. One in particular, Joseph Saunders, had expanded the works, building a factory and a dye-house behind it. The trouble began when another clothier, Joseph Phelps, took over. By 1788, he was developing the scribbling horse. Machines do not need paying, they don't riot, and they work where you want them to, not at home, as many weavers and spinners did. Clothiers and master weavers were keen to introduce them wherever possible. The skilled craftsmen saw that if this came about, they would be out of work and starving. They were determined not to let that happen.

An angry crowd of about 500 people gathered outside Westbury House, demanding that Phelps hand over the scribbling horse or promise not to use it any more. Phelps refused, so the sticks and stones began to fly. Eventually Phelps and some friends opened fire. It says much for the determination of the angry crowd outside that even with dead and injured comrades around them, they persisted in their demands. Phelps was finally obliged to hand over the scribbling horse, which was burnt in triumph on the town bridge. It was an empty victory, for progress, whether for good or ill, is an unstoppable juggernaut. The machines eventually replaced skilled craftsmen long before the west country trade lost out to the great factories of the north. At the inquest on the man, woman and boy who were killed by Phelps's action, the coroner declared it to be justifiable homicide. Phelps, however, was not the only one to get off scot-free. Four of the rioters,

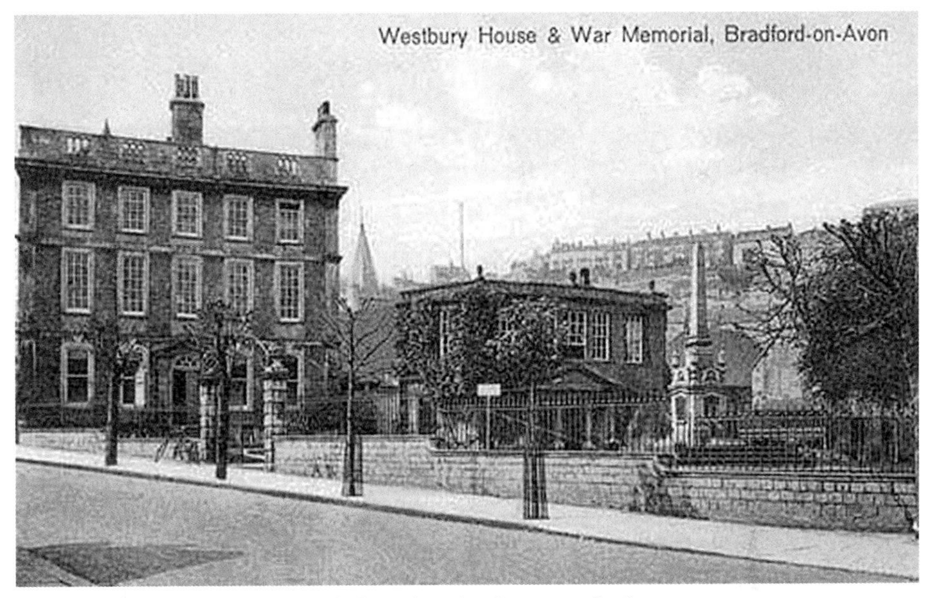

It was from one of these windows that the shots were fired. Author's collection

Samuel Norman, James Bryant, William Greenland, and Benjamin Derrett, were subsequently arrested and committed for trial at the assizes. Against Derrett no bill was found and the rest were acquitted.

John Butler of Bath, had not been so lucky, eleven years earlier. Susan Burney wrote a letter to her sister Fanny on 8 June 1780, describing her terror at the anti-Catholic riots in London. By the time the letter arrived Fanny was all too well aware of what they were like, as a similar riot had broken out in Bath just one day later. The seeds of the trouble lay with an act passed in 1778, relieving Catholics of all the restrictions and demands which had been placed upon them. Today that would seem a humane and just act, which is how it was viewed by progressive minds in the eighteenth century (although the government had an ulterior motive – to make it easy for Roman Catholics to enlist in the fight against the American colonists). Unfortunately, there were a considerable number of extreme Protestants who violently objected, particularly in Scotland, where the law was not yet in force. By going on to the streets in Edinburgh and Glasgow, they persuaded the Government not to extend the law to Scotland. This inspired Protestant extremists in England, and they turned to an eccentric MP, Lord George Gordon. He came from a Scottish family, with many Catholic members, although he was rabidly Protestant. His family had, as author Christopher Hibbert delicately puts it, 'for generations shown occasional signs of something more than eccen-

Despite the riots, machines such as these took over from the skilled weavers. Now they too are museum pieces – as here in Trowbridge. Andrew Swift

tricity', although much of the criticism levelled at him throughout his career was due to his ability to empathise with the common man. Thrown out of the navy for being too much on the side of the lower decks, he turned to politics. It was said of him that there were three parties in Parliament, Whigs, Tories and Lord George Gordon. It was to him that the Protestants of England turned to get the hated act repealed. Had they known what was to ensue, they might have thought again.

Gordon decided to take a petition to parliament at the head of a crowd of 50,000 followers. Needless to say, the disaffected, the poor, and the simply lawless joined in and an orgy of destruction began. Only two cities were seriously affected, however. One was London, where the riots went on for a week. The other was Bath. This was completely unexpected, because Bath had always had a very relaxed and liberal attitude to Catholics. Their place of worship was even shown on maps of the city, which was quite remarkable for the time. Yet anti-Catholic feeling was simmering below the surface in some quarters, although Fanny Burney refused to believe the rumours she had heard – such things did not occur in Bath – they would be

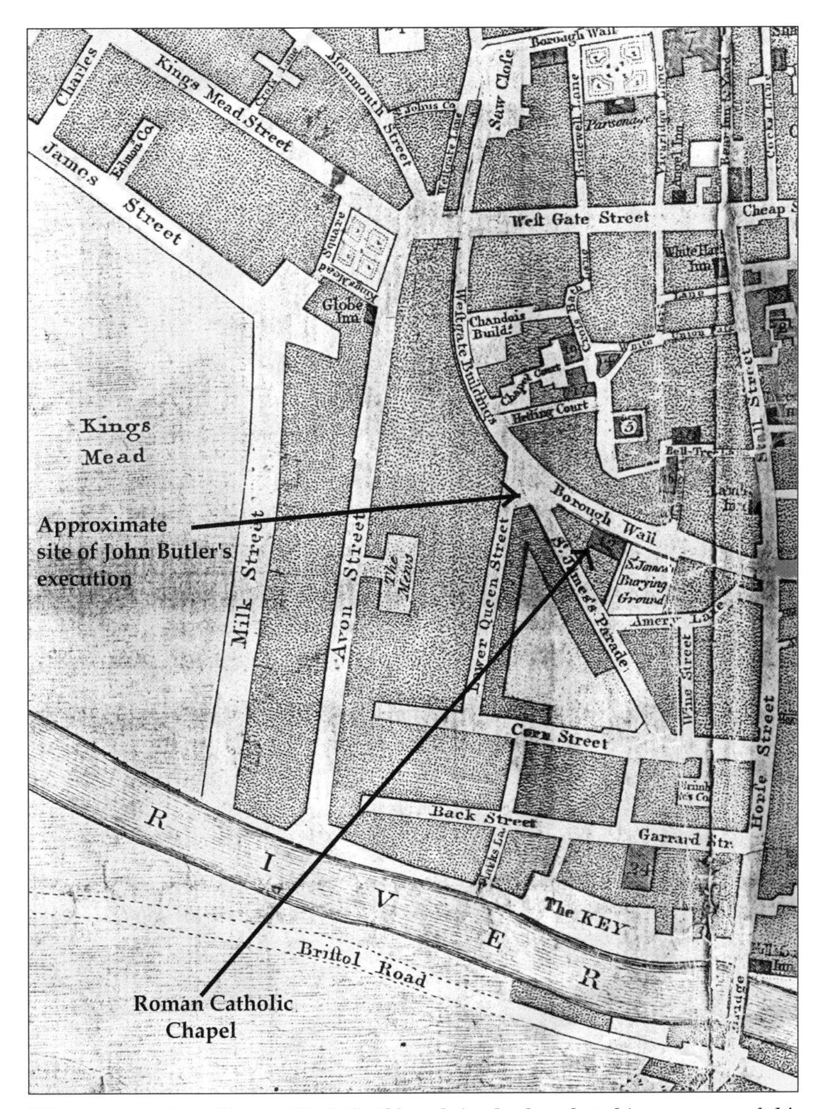

The presence of the Roman Catholic Chapel (and other chapels) on a map of this date shows how liberal Bath was in its attitude to religion. Most towns only recognised the Church of England. Author's collection

injurious to the health of the poor invalids! She was wrong. On the night of Friday 9 June, trouble erupted.

The *Bath Chronicle* takes up the story:

> Friday evening a most alarming riot happened here, which was begun by a footman and some boys breaking the windows of a house where the Roman Catholic priest resided, adjoining to a new Chapel, newly built for

persons of that religion. In a very short time, as night came on, they were joined by a great number of people, most of them strangers, and armed with carpenter's tools, who broke open the chapel doors immediately and began gutting it and throwing the materials out of the window. The Magistrates and other peace officers assembled as quick as possible, but ere they could exert themselves the mob had increased to such a multitude that every effort to disperse them was ineffectual. The riot act was read and some persons seized, but instantly rescued. The Magistrates and many respectable citizens used every possible exertion to prevail on the mob to disperse, but without effect. Major Molesworth with a few of the City Volunteers hastily collected went into the Chapel, to the imminent hazard of their lives, and so far prevailed with the rioters as to be suffered to put out the fire several times, which they repeatedly kindled for its destruction. About 20 more of the Volunteers were soon after got together, and Capt. Duperre, at the request of the Mayor, headed them and led them into the Chapel, with their pieces not loaded. The instant they entered the building the mob rushed in upon them on all sides, and a pistol was fired at Capt. Duperre, which fortunately missed, and as fortunately destroyed an old rioter who had been once before wounded at an insurrection at Trowbridge – but it so incensed the mob, who supposed him shot by one of the Volunteers, that they immediately fired the Chapel, and the corps having received a few wounds and finding it utterly impossible to resist so large a body, made a slow and good retreat. The Chapel and about six or seven houses that surrounded it were entirely burnt by about four in the morning, when this desperate rabble, by the repeated and laudable exertions of the Magistrates and citizens, were prevailed upon to disperse, without carrying the remainder of their diabolical plan into execution, they having declared their determination to fire the old chapel and the houses of several Roman Catholics residing here.

As soon as the Mayor and Corporation saw the impossibility of so numerous and desperate a mob being quelled by the civil power, amounting to some thousands, they sent expresses to Wells, Devizes, etc., and to the Commanding Officers of the troops there to come to their assistance . . . It is impossible to say too much in commendation of all the officers both horse and foot for their uncommon expedition on this occasion. They understood from the messengers that the town was fired in several places, and how desperate and large a body they were to encounter, which the flames they saw from the neighbouring hills seemed to confirm – yet the danger only served to hasten them to our relief. Most of the Corporation stayed up all night to watch the city and receive the officers at their arrival, whom they very properly invited to an elegant dinner. By the disposition of the troops and peace officers everything here now is perfectly quiet. It is universally agreed that the leaders in the riot were persons sent from London, the gutting and firing the Chapel was executed with amazing haste and regularity, and not a single person in the city was insulted except those who attempted to seize them.

Fanny Burney. Author's collection

Fear and consternation spread through the city. Fanny Burney, whose own family had only just escaped the mob in London thanks to her father's quick thinking, was staying with the Thrales in South Parade. Though not Catholic themselves, Mr Thrale was known to be a Catholic sympathiser and his house and brewery at Streatham were considered to be possible targets. Two days after the riot in Bath, they fled to Brighton, even though Bath was by now almost under military rule, the Mayor having acted a great deal more decisively than the Lord Mayor of London. Having got on top of the situation, the authorities in Bath were determined that someone should be a scapegoat – and that scapegoat was a footman who worked for the City architect, Thomas Baldwin. His name was John Butler. The *Bath Chronicle* reported his trial in full:

> John Butler was arraigned at half past nine [on Friday 30 August]. He was indicted for that he and others (twenty more) unlawfully assembled on the 9th of June and began to demolish the house of John Brewer in the Parish of St James. The second count charged him with beginning to destroy an out-house of the said Mr Brewer.

Mr Batt shortly opened the indictment, after which Serjeant Davy went into the case fully. He began with lamenting the late riots, which threatened not only Government itself, but the whole society at large. What induced the prisoner to take the part he did, he could not say, but would, from charity, suppose he was actuated by a zeal for the Protestant religion.

There was, he observed, a reciprocal duty between the King and the subject: the subject owed allegiance to the Crown, and the Crown protection to the people; the people, if they do not pay allegiance to the Crown, are not intitled to protection. In the present case, the Crown was not able to afford the protection to be wished. The riots began in London, and were too great to be suppressed by the Civil Magistrates; this made it necessary for the King to call in the aid of the military. Bath being a place of resort for the sick or for pleasure, there was no military there: Government had never quartered any there, and therefore riots there are more alarming than in other places; a riot there ought to be immediately attended to, and the perpetrators punished. There are two considerations: First, the story of what happened at Bath; second, the share the prisoner took in it. The Serjeant then proceeded to state the particulars of the late riot at Bath, and the share the prisoner took, who, he informed the jury, was perhaps the first instigator, by huzzaing, waving his hat, and crying, 'no Popery, down with Popery,' at the head of the mob, pursuing

This elegant scene is very different from the night when the terrified Mr Brewer ran up the High Street, pursued by an angry mob. He passed in front of the houses in the distance, running from right to left, turned up into the market place, was turned away from the Guildhall (centre of picture) and took refuge in the White Lion *(at left).* Bath Central Library

Mr Brewer, who is a Romish Priest, through the streets, till he ran into a house for protection and was driven out, and from thence pursued to the gates of the Guildhall, where he found protection. [This was wrong. In fact he had been turned away from the Guildhall and took refuge in the White Lion Inn next door.] Butler began with his own hand by throwing stones, and when he had done this, left the mob to complete the business he had begun.

If any were eminently to be distinguished from others, it was the man who first incited, who first began, and who first stirred up, the mob to do the mischiefs which afterwards were effected. Butler was a footman, and, till this affair, his character, he believed, was untainted. The Serjeant next observed, that in treason and riots, like those stated in the indictment, character was of no use, but in other common charges, such as sheep-stealing, etc., character might go a great way. If the accusation be proved to be true, the jury would discharge their duty by finding him guilty; if not, the Serjeant said he should rejoice with the best and warmest of the prisoner's friends in their acquitting him.

Samuel Wheeler deposed that he knew the prisoner and saw him in the evening of the 9th of June, in his master's house, between six and seven. The witness lived with Mr Baldwin in the Crescent, was footman there, and was speaking with the prisoner of the riots in London. The prisoner asked him how the affairs went on in London, he told him he heard chapels were demolished. The witness said it was a pity chapels were demolished. The prisoner said it was no matter whether the chapels were demolished or not. The witness thought it a pity in such troublesome times. The prisoner said he supposed the witness was a Roman Catholic. The witness replied, 'it is no matter what religion I am of; I am no Roman Catholic.' The witness saw him again about half past eight, in Pierrepoint Street, afterwards in the Market Place going homewards, but saw him in no other street; when he saw him in Pierrepoint Street he was with a parcel of boys, about 30 or 40, crying, 'No Popery.' He believed the prisoner cried, 'No Popery,' but could not distinguish his voice from the rest. He did not see him wave his hat. They were chiefly boys or between boys and men.

John Cottell said he lived in Stall Street and was a shoemaker by trade. A little after eight in the evening on the 9th of June, he saw the prisoner at his door, but the first time he saw him he was coming down Belltree Lane [Beau Street]. Mr Brewer was before him, the prisoner behind. The witness went down to the bottom of the Alms Lane, where the building was, which was afterwards destroyed; he saw many people, among whom was his journeyman and others removing their goods. When he got into Stall Street, he saw Mr Brewer running along the lane and into Stall Street, the prisoner following him with 30 or 40 boys with him. Mr Brewer ran into his shop, the witness followed him; he said he came in for fear of the people. The witness asked him what was the matter, for he seemed much frightened by the people before his door; he asked him to walk into the parlour, which he did; the witness went from the parlour to the door and said to the prisoner, 'for God's sake, what do you want, you don't want to murder the man?' The prisoner said, 'you are no Roman Catholic, turn the Popish son of a bitch out.' He had his hat waving in his hand and cried, 'No Popery;' then it seemed general among the whole mob, 'turn him out, turn him out;' he thought it in vain his speaking to them, as they did not go away. He then returned to the parlour to Mr Brewer, who, having heard what passed, went out at the same door he came in, and went up the street, and the prisoner with the mob followed him. Mr Brewer ran as far as he could see him, which was halfway up the street, all crying 'No Popery,' the prisoner and all cried so; he then lost sight of him, and in a few minutes the prisoner returned, running very fast, and the boys with him, but not so many as before; they came down Belltree Lane and were running towards the chapel.

John Horton, Chief Constable, deposed, that he saw the prisoner between eight and nine o'clock coming down Westgate Street with 30 or 40 boys and grown people; that he came huzzaing, waving his hat and crying, 'No Popery.' The witness went to him, and asked him the meaning of those people being there, and told him, 'twould be attended with bad consequences, and productive of much mischief; bade him go home and mind his business; he made no answer, but cried, 'No Popery,' and repeated it two or three times; he spoke to him again, and one of the men jostled him and his brother officer, Mr Smith; he then said again to the prisoner, 'you don't know the consequence that will arise, it may be very fatal to the town.' The prisoner said, 'you will know more by and by,' then waved his hat, huzzaed, cried, 'No Popery,' and went away towards St James's Parade and towards the Chapel; the mob followed him to the amount of 50, 60, 70, much increased.

Charles Davis deposed that he saw the prisoner on the 9th of June in the afternoon, between three and four o'clock, blowing a fife, and walking slow, no mob about him then. Between eight and nine in the evening, in Cheap Street, opposite the opening to the Churchyard, he saw Mr Brewer running, and the prisoner and boys following him, very quick; the witness then went home, and had not been there above ten minutes, before he heard a noise at the Romish Chapel, and boys breaking the windows at the east end with stones, dirt, etc., that there were between 50 and 100 people. He went from the crowd to endeavour to get some constables to suppress the riot; the prisoner was very active running about among them, seeming to encourage them, had his hat in his hand, and was huzzaing. The witness was away a quarter of an hour for assistance; when he returned he saw the mob very active in breaking open the doors; that he saw the door broke open, and immediately some returned with benches and other things into the street; that they went on from that time progressively in destroying everything; that there was a communication from the Chapel to Mr Brewer's house, through which he believes the mob got; that after burning the furniture, etc., in the street, the Chapel and five dwelling houses were set fire to and burnt. The Mayor came about eleven o'clock, and the volunteers to the number of 20 or 30 men, but they were not sufficient to disperse the mob; that the prisoner was very active, waving his hat and huzzaing.

Cross examined – he never saw the prisoner after his return; the last time he saw him was when the boys were breaking windows; he did not see him at the time of the fire.

William Tucker deposed that (standing with Mr Davis) he saw the prisoner on the 9th of June between three and four o'clock in the afternoon, playing a fife in a blue livery, as he passed Westgate Buildings; that he played horribly bad, which made them notice it; about nine in the evening he heard a noise in the street and saw the prisoner, but not Brewer. He heard some people say, there's the man hunting the priest; that he seemed to be at the head of some boys, waving his hand, but could not hear him say anything because he was not near enough; that he heard a noise at the Chapel about ten minutes after, went down, and saw the prisoner at the head of some boys, standing upon some mortar or rising ground to make himself conspicuous, waving his hat and crying out, 'No Popery,' while the boys were breaking the windows; saw no man take any active part, but saw a boy throw a stone and knock him down, and said, 'what do you do here?,' when he was immediately surrounded by three, or four, or six men, in carmen's frocks; two or three of them said, 'you had better go away, or you will be used ill;' that he took their advice and went away, leaving the prisoner still on the same rising ground; he returned to the place again in about four or five minutes, but did not see the prisoner; the mob had increased, the windows were broke, and the door either was broke open, or they were breaking it open, and were taking out the benches, etc., and making heaps in the street; that he saw a variety of household furniture burnt on St James's Parade, and that the Chapel and houses were afterwards burnt.

Cross examined – he saw nothing of the prisoner after his return and does not know whether the prisoner was there when the house was broke open.

Thomas Baldwin, architect, deposed, that he saw the prisoner between half after ten and twelve o'clock near the Chapel; the people were then pulling down the house, that the prisoner was then 60 yards from them, standing as an idle spectator, and the mob destroying the cornice.

Cross examined – he said he could not speak to any other time than from half past ten to twelve; the witness did not stay there above two or three minutes; that the mob extended a great way, and he was near the prisoner when they were pulling down the cornice.

Mary Hughes deposed that on the 9th of June she saw the prisoner in the Churchyard near the Pump Room and several boys with him, all following Mr Brewer, who was running as fast as he could, the mob all crying out, 'knock him down,' but she would not swear that the prisoner said it, without she had heard him alone; there were three or four people between the prisoner and Mr Brewer. Mr Brewer ran by her very fast and tore her gown; she was much frightened, stayed to rest, and something after nine went towards the Chapel and saw the prisoner there, huzzaing, and a great number hammering at the door; the prisoner waved his hat and huzzaed, but she did not see the prisoner do anything. She did not see Davis or Tucker there.

Mr Hennagan deposed that he had known the prisoner a year, saw him first in the Market Place, and heard him huzza; there were many people with him between eight and nine o'clock; that he saw no more of the prisoner till he saw him at the Chapel, which was five or six minutes after the mob had broke the windows by throwing stones; that he saw the prisoner opposite a blacksmith's shop near the Chapel, and saw him throw some stones or brickbats at it; he saw him heave two stones, cannot speak positively to more, is perfectly sure of the person of the man, but cannot say whether the stones reached the building.

John Ridley deposed that on the 9th of June he saw the prisoner about a quarter before nine o'clock, at a building adjoining the Romish Chapel, boys breaking the windows, throwing volleys of stones, the prisoner huzzaed with them, and encouraged them, standing on a lump of mortar, and said, 'fire away, boys,' that he was there till he saw the peace-officers with their staves, and saw the prisoner then run away.

Cross examined – he ran away before the house door broke open, a little before nine or about nine.

Mr William Robinson, architect, deposed, that he built a long room called a Chapel; that the communication between the Chapel and the dwelling house was by three doors, one below, two above stairs; all one building, all carried up together, and all in Brewer's possession; he saw it after the fire, all the carpenter's work consumed, walls greatly damaged, windows and doors destroyed, and nothing but walls remaining.

Cross examined – Mr Brewer was understood to be the person to officiate there; the room was intended for a Chapel to perform divine service, and no other purpose; and the gallery for the purpose of coming into the Chapel ....

For The Prisoner

Elizabeth Rickets: 'I live with Mr Baldwin; on the 9th of June I saw the prisoner come in at a quarter past nine, and laid the cloth for supper, waited at supper, and went to bed twenty minutes before eleven; he was never out of the house after he came in at a quarter past nine.'

Cross Examination: No apprehension that he would be arrested, no other particular reason than laying the cloth for remembering; when he went upstairs to bed, she went after him and looked at the clock, took exact notice, and generally looks at the clock when she goes to bed; her master and mistress generally go to bed after, but cannot say when they went to bed. She left nobody up but her master and mistress and the housekeeper; she took more notice that night of the hour than ever she did before: she is sure it was exactly twenty minutes, and that he went out at half past eight, and came home at a quarter past nine; he was not out all the afternoon, but with a letter to the post between four and five, and returned in half an hour. The family dined in the parlour at three, and then the prisoner dined with the servants, and it was after four when he put the things away, and then went with the letter, and was not away more than half an hour, and then was not out any more till half past eight, and returned at a quarter past nine. He was never out all the day or night but in going to the post office, and from half past eight till a quarter past nine, and never out after supper. It is about half a mile from the Crescent to the Chapel and post office near there, and is very sure it was full half an hour past eight before he went out in the evening.

Mrs Jane Powell, housekeeper: About four o'clock, the prisoner went to the post office, was away half an hour, she thought he made haste. At half past eight, he went out, she looked at her watch, as she was going out herself; she did not come in till 20 minutes before ten; he was then in. At half past eleven, people said he was at the head of a mob; she went up to his bedroom and called, 'John, are you abed?' He answered, 'yes.' He said no more, nor she said no more. She looked into the room again about twelve, her mistress desired her to go up, telling her that she had heard he was in the mob; that she met her master, told him of it, and that he went up himself to see. She was sure the prisoner was not out after supper.

Mr Baldwin was from six to ten o'clock on the 9th of June on a visit at a neighbour's house; he returned at ten; the prisoner let him in at the door; his wife had done supper; a Lady told him there had been a great confusion, that he went out to see the place and returned in half an hour. Supposed, notice had been given a day or two before, there would be a riot, to the magistrates. That his wife told him somebody had said his servant was in the mob; that he understood it was a message from Mr Wiltshire to him, and said he went upstairs at eleven and saw him in bed; that he did not remember the maid's speaking to him on the stairs or meeting her. The prisoner had lived with him between two and three years; was sober, civil, diligent, and honest, and that he had never had a more valuable servant in his life. That he went to bed between one and two; did not know whether any of the servants were at the door, but that the housekeeper sat up till all were abed.

Rev Mr Pearce had known the prisoner twelve years; gave him a good character; he had lived with him two years.

Mr James Haynes gave him a good character, as a sober, honest servant, and never out one night while in his service, or given to riot or quarrel. A written character was produced and read, of a gentleman with whom he had lived some years, speaking very respectfully of him.

The learned Judge here summed up the evidence with great candour and impartiality, making very pointed and apt observations on the whole of it. The Jury, after five minutes conversation, found the prisoner guilty; but recommended him to mercy.

The trial lasted from nine in the morning till three in the afternoon.

The jury might have recommended mercy but, even on the confused and contradictory evidence, Butler was not about to get it. Curiously, the seven men who were charged with him were all acquitted. Most pleaded that they had simply got involved because they were bullied into joining the protest. Butler, if indeed it was he leading the charge, had no such excuse. One prisoner, Peter Butcher, had even been seen at the chapel by two reliable witnesses, but the jury preferred to believe Butcher's drinking companions. Butler, however, was sentenced to death. It was a draconian sentence. Terrifying though the experience had been for Mr Brewer, the only death had been that of the old man accidentally shot by one of his fellow rioters. The council, clearly expecting more trouble, acted with speed. Only three days after the verdict was delivered, a gallows was erected on a piece of waste land outside the city wall, just yards from the ruins of Mr Brewer's chapel. At lunchtime, a melancholy procession, made up of Butler on a cart, almost in a state of collapse and supported by his two brothers, followed by 400 special constables, wound its way from the prison in Grove Street to the place of execution. Just in case anyone was thinking of protesting, the Scots Greys and the Bath Volunteer regiment were drawn up ready for action in Queen Square. Butler prayed with a clergyman, Reverend Philipps, for half an hour, and the clergyman then read out a letter which the young man had written just before he left the prison. In it he swore once again that he had returned to his master's house at a quarter past nine, and not left it until after eleven o'clock the next morning. The hanging took place amid crowds of weeping spectators. John Butler was just twenty-six years old.

Lord George Gordon, on the other hand, was acquitted of treason at his trial, but the system got him in the end. In 1786 he was found guilty of libel against Marie Antoinette but fled abroad to Amsterdam, where he converted to Judaism. He was later discovered living in the Jewish quarter of Birmingham, having returned secretly. He was sent to Newgate, but when his sentence was up, he refused to give sureties of his good behaviour, and was returned to prison. He contracted prison fever, and died at the age of forty-two. His hotheadedness, far from furthering the cause of the common man, had meant that middle class campaigners drew back from militant action. Successful revolutions occur when the middle classes become disaffected, and after 1780 England's bourgeoisie was horrified at the possible outcome. There would never be an English Revolution. There would also never be the same level of unrest on the streets of Bath, but that did not mean that life was entirely peaceful. In 1800, Williams' Brewery at the Quay was burnt down, and threatening letters made it clear this was no accidental fire. There was mass unemployment at the time, and many of the poor were starving.

In 1817, a potentially explosive situation passed off peacefully, when the noted political activist, Henry 'Orator' Hunt held a public meeting in his yard at Walcot Street to campaign for universal male suffrage. Numbers were so great that the meeting had to move to the Orange Grove. Once again the Mayor had sworn in special constables and called in the army, in the shape of two troops of the 23rd Dragoons, four troops of the North Somerset Yeomanry and the Bath

Mr Hunt's yard as it appears today, with the tramshed of 1903 converted to upmarkets flats and a trendy bar. Andrew Swift

Rifle Corps. If the staunchly right-wing *Bath Chronicle* was right in its assessment of only 500 people being present, this seems like overkill, but of course, the number was far greater. Hunt claimed 10,000–12,000, and even if this was an overestimate, it was still an impressive gathering. Fortunately, the crowd dispersed without trouble, largely due to the Mayor and the army keeping calm and taking no action. When Hunt went to address a meeting in St Peter's Fields in Manchester, two years later, 80,000 were present and the military charged the crowd to disperse it. Eleven people died and over 400 were wounded. It went down in history as the Massacre of Peterloo. It could so easily have happened in the centre of Bath.

It was Bristol's turn for mass destruction in 1831, with the Corn Law Riots. The Bristol magistrates called for assistance, and Captain Wilkins of Twerton turned up in Bath to gather up the men of the Bath troop of the Yeomanry Cavalry. Wilkins was something of a reformer himself, despite being an industrialist, but he believed in law and order. When he rested at the *White Hart*, in Stall Street, the mob began to gather, to persuade him, by force if necessary, not to go. He pointed out that he was compelled, as a matter of duty, to ride to

The White Hart, *Stall Street, in its heyday.* Author's collection

Bristol, and despite various attempts to make him change his mind, he continued to make it clear that he, and the troop, were going. Some of the crowd tried to follow him into the inn, but the doors were closed in their faces. The mob then mounted an attack on the inn, smashing the windows. The shutters were closed, so the mob went and fetched pieces of wood to smash them, and some managed to break in. Here a rude shock awaited them. One of Wilkins' men worked at the inn as a chef, and he had the idea of heating up kitchen pokers till they were red hot, as a means of defence. The invaders beat a hasty retreat, during which the pokers were enthusiastically applied to a tender if well-padded part of their anatomies. By this time, 300 hastily sworn–in constables had made their appearance, and the mob was dispersed, although they later took their revenge on two other inns owned by the proprietors of the *White Hart*. Two of the rioters were later sentenced to death, but this time their sentences were commuted to transportation for life.

In 1832, the first Reform Act introduced a measure of male suffrage into the system, although the property qualifications meant that it only covered the nobility and the upper middle classes – and no women were allowed to vote at all. What is more, the vote was not secret. This meant that intimidation of voters was rife, and unscrupulous politicians had no qualms about turning to the mob as 'persuaders'. The year 1841 saw the Drunken Election in Bath. That it should have received such a name in an age when drunkenness was endemic, and paying one's supporters in drink was common, gives some idea of just how bad things were. (It is also noteworthy that by this time the parties were the Liberals and the Conservatives, their colours being the same as today.) Two Liberals, Roebuck and Duncan, were standing in a city noted for its conservatism, and their supporters were determined they should get in. Oddly enough, although most of the violence was drink fuelled, many publicans were Conservatives, so pubs took the brunt of the attacks. Avon Street, which was noted for its brothels and pubs, saw a violent attack on the *Crown and Thistle*, for example, when doors and windows were smashed and property stolen. During the attack, an old man wearing blue colours was struck and knocked into the passage.

Roebuck and Duncan were duly elected, but six years later Roebuck lost his seat to Lord Ashley. This nobleman, foolishly as it turned out, announced proudly that 'not a penny during the last six months was expended on beer'. The mob was outraged – politicians of whatever colour were expected to buy beer for the disenfranchised. The angry crowd attacked any houses in the genteel streets where Ashley's supporters lived. North and South Parades were visited, and a house in Milsom Street was left windowless. After refreshing themselves at the radical *Gloucester Inn* on treble-X beer the crowd headed for Cleveland Bridge. Here the toll-keeper was forced to open the tollgate and they continued along Bathwick Street, smashing windows at another supporter's hose before climbing Bathwick Hill. Assuming that anyone who lived there was likely to be a Conservative, they

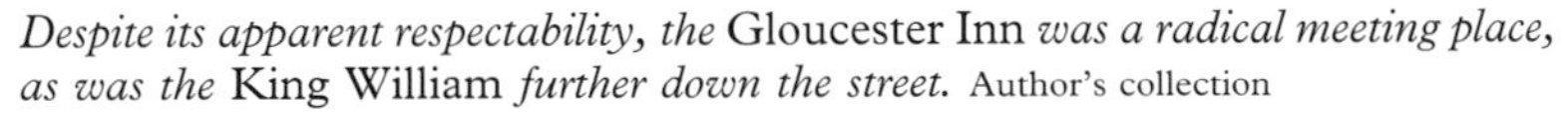
Despite its apparent respectability, the Gloucester Inn *was a radical meeting place, as was the* King William *further down the street.* Author's collection

Despite Bathwick Hill House's seclusion, its lodge-house (right) and formidable gates, the determined mob marched up this driveway to smash its windows. Andrew Swift

smashed windows as they went, until they reached Bathwick Hill House, the home of W T Blair, one of Ashley's most prominent supporters. The havoc they wreaked here was described in the newspaper as 'very great indeed' which, given what they had achieved elsewhere, seems likely to have been an understatement. It was the last disorderly election, however. As suffrage was extended, secret ballots were introduced, and drinking itself became a political issue, such demonstrations at election time disappeared.

It took longer, however, for Avon Street to become respectable. *The Fountain*, Avon Street's largest pub, was particularly prone to trouble. In 1849, a man called James Tiley was ejected by force from the pub for being objectionable (and in Avon Street he must have been behaving outrageously for the publican to sit up and take notice). Tiley's friends took exception to this and came to his aid. Once out on the street, Tiley smashed some of the windows with his fist. Meanwhile, the police had been called, and they chased Tiley down the street. Aided by his friends he took refuge in the house of woman called McDonald, and here the police met determined resistance. The inmates attacked them with pikes and sticks, while outside the mob joined in defending Tiley. The police had to abandon their attempt to capture Tiley, although they did succeed in arresting the woman.

Less than three years later, *The Fountain* was again the scene of street disturbances, but this time the mob, ever fickle, was on the side of law and order. One Saturday night, an Irishman called Richard Barratt had committed an outrage (unspecified, although a number of possibilities come to mind) at an upstairs window, and was threatening the mob. A woman with him then threw a lump of coal down on the irate crowd. Once again the window was smashed, at which Barratt rushed out of the house 'furiously wielding a poker, and followed people down the street, attempting to strike indiscriminately as he proceeded'. He must have been a very impressive figure to make the people of Avon Street turn and run, but he was later arrested and charged with being drunk and disorderly.

It may not seem like it at times, but when we look at stories like these, we realise that Bath is much more law-abiding that it was just 150 years ago.

CHAPTER 5

Murder Most Foul

Violent death in Bath in the eighteenth, nineteenth, and twentieth centuries

Throughout the centuries Bath's guidebooks have tried to persuade would-be visitors that this was definitely the place to come – delightful, fashionable, and safe. As we have already seen, there was another side to this story and the city has not been a stranger to crime of many kinds. But murder is rarer. In this chapter we look at three murders, in three different centuries.

The eighteenth century – the shooting of Maria Bally

Avon Street and Corn Street, although built in the early eighteenth century as respectable lodging-houses, soon lost their air of gentility. They were built too close to the river. Not only did the river flood with monotonous regularity, it was filthy dirty, a place where horses were washed and watered, boats plied a regular trade, and into which sewers emptied. The area became home to some of the poorest in Bath, including prostitutes, second-hand clothes dealers, as well as some perfectly respectable artisans who could not afford to have premises elsewhere. It seems to have been an act of Christian charity which persuaded a hairdresser and perfumer from Milsom Street to open a day school in Corn Street in 1794. It was an act of kindness for which she would pay with her life. Her name was Maria Bally, and she had been brought up by her uncle, a non-conformist clergyman. She was nineteen years old, with a pleasing manner, and had a beautiful if placid countenance. More importantly, she was due to inherit some property when she came of age. Not surprisingly, when her uncle went to religious meetings, his niece went too, and there she met a young journeyman shoemaker called William White. He was twenty-two, well brought up and described as religious. What the newspaper of the time described as 'a mutual regard' developed between them. What Maria did not know was that quiet, pious William was also passionate and possessive. If he could not have her, no one else would.

Just before Christmas 1794, William went up to London and he bought a brace of brass pocket pistols, telling the shopkeeper that he needed them to protect his property. Since he had virtually no property (he lived in lodgings) the property he had in mind seems to have been Maria. On his return to Bath, he continued his courtship, but there were beginning to be quarrels. They were only slight, but all the indications are that Maria was starting to have a bad feeling about her suitor. White continued to talk of marriage and told his friends that he was finding rooms for the couple to live after their wedding. Meanwhile, Maria's doubts grew. She was sure he had been lying to her over various things, and she finally rejected him. The scene was now set for what would be a terrifying experience for the children of Corn Street.

William White made preparations for revenge. Redeeming his pistols from the pawnbroker, where he had deposited them on his return from London, he made some ammunition by melting lead in the bowl of his tobacco pipe. (It was not uncommon at this time to make one's own lead shot.) Although unused to alcohol, he gave himself Dutch courage by drinking one pint of strong beer and two glasses of brandy and set out for Corn Street.

It was now between ten and eleven o'clock on 9 June. The children were sitting quietly in the schoolroom in Corn Street, which Maria Bally had rented in a lodging-house. What happened next is slightly muddled, as the only eyewitness to appear at the inquest was the

A glimpse of Corn Street – most of this has now gone and is at present a car park while it awaits redevelopment plans. Bath Central Library

seven-and-a-half-year-old Elizabeth Champion. She was probably called because she seems to have been the quickest child to react sensibly to the disaster. White entered the room and sat down at a small distance from Maria Bally. He continued sitting there, but Elizabeth reported she suddenly heard the sound of a pistol being fired and saw the smoke of the powder. Miss Bally fell from her chair on to the floor. Elizabeth saw blood on the left side of her teacher's head, just above her ear, and immediately left the room, followed by the other children, to get assistance. She ran over to the house of Fanny Greenslade, who lived across the road, and told her that a man her killed her Ma'am.

Fanny Greenslade said she had seen William White enter the house where Maria Bally was and shortly afterwards heard a gunshot. Almost immediately Elizabeth appeared at her door, telling her what had happened and, as she went into the street, the rest of the children ran out, crying 'Murder!' With the children came White himself, whereupon Fanny asked him what he had done. He held out the pistol in his hand and said: 'Take me. I yield myself.'

The next witness to be called was John Lacey, a shoemaker, who had lodgings in the same house as the schoolroom, on the floor above. Hearing the pistol shot, he ran downstairs, to find White coming out the room with a pistol in each hand, one of them discharged. Another lodger in the house, Adrian Abbott, a cabinet-maker, was passing through the passageway when he saw the crowd of people outside Maria Bally's room. William White, who seemed to be having trouble getting someone to arrest him – since he was armed this is not perhaps surprising – came up to Abbott and said: 'I want to surrender myself to justice. I want the justice of the law to take place upon me for I have killed her.' He then handed over the loaded pistol from his coat pocket (the other presumably now in the possession of Fanny Greenslade) and surrendered himself to Abbott.

Given all this evidence and the fact that White himself freely admitted the murder, the outcome of the trial was inevitable. He was found guilty of wilful murder and sentenced to death. The story attracted a great deal of public notice, and a huge crowd gathered to watch the hanging. After praying for half an hour with a clergyman, White addressed the throng for another twenty minutes, quoting a lengthy poem by Dr Edward Young, entitled *The Complaint, or Night Thoughts on Life, Death and Mortality*. He concluded with advice to be careful how one formed connections and not to trifle with other people's feelings, before being despatched from this earth.

In the report in the Bath Chronicle of the trial and execution, there is a distinct sense that White was being badly treated, and that in some way Miss Bally was to blame. Why should this be? Today, we would recognise William White as having all the classic attributes of a stalker, but, to conservative elements in Bath, Miss Bally may have been seen as rather subversive. She belonged to a nonconformist church, she had been well-educated and, alarmingly to many, she was prepared to educate the masses. Since many in authority considered that the less literate the masses were the better, on the grounds that education might cause them to be dissatisfied with their lot, Maria Bally would not have been regarded with approval. In our next story, however, from the nineteenth century, the victims are regarded throughout with sympathy. This time the murder took place not in the rough and tumble of Avon Street but in the rarefied atmosphere of Lansdown. The victim was once again an educated and determined woman, but the killer was not a lover but her own father.

The nineteenth century – the father's revenge

No. 1 Spencer's Belle Vue is an unremarkable Georgian house in a terrace on Lansdown Hill, near both Lansdown and Camden Crescents – the country where Jane Austen herself would sometimes

No. 1 Spencer's Belle Vue today. The author

stroll. But the events of August 1870 were far removed from any novel by Jane Austen. No. 1 was home to a widowed schoolmaster, John Prankerd and his four daughters but, as the evidence later showed, it was far from a happy home for the four girls, the youngest of whom was described by the *Bath Chronicle* as an imbecile. The two eldest, Mary (known as Minnie) and Kate were twenty-two and nineteen years old respectively, while the other two were fifteen and thirteen. Evidence was given at the inquest that Mr Prankerd was in the habit of ill-treating his daughters, on one occasion breaking a water-vessel over one of the girls' head. The servant, Ellen Davis, had seen him strike Minnie and pull her hair. Kate also bore signs of mistreatment. By August 1870, Minnie had had enough, and she secured for herself the post of governess for a family living on the continent. To say her father was angry about this was an understatement. There had been

Genteel Lansdown hit the headlines of the Police Gazette *in 1870, along with two other gruesome murders, and a suicide.* Bath Central Library

several altercations between herself and her father, but she had continued with her packing and making preparations for her departure despite his opposition.

The servant – Ellen Davis – was the first witness at the inquest. She told the jury she had been in post for three years. Three daughters were living at home at the time of the tragedy – the fate of the fourth remained a cause for concern for a little while, but she was eventually found safe. On the day in question, the school, which was held in the house, was closed for the holidays, and Prankerd left home very early. He was not expected home by his daughters until two in the afternoon. The youngest, the one described as an imbecile, was with Ellen in the kitchen, while the fifteen-year-old had been taken away by her father the previous week, to an unknown destination. Prankerd returned earlier than expected. His daughters were out, but he did not ask after them. Instead, he asked Ellen if she would like a trip. She asked what he meant and he said she could go away by train for the afternoon. She answered: 'No, sir: I have nowhere to go.' To this he retorted that she could go to Taunton, but Ellen, who did not say so but seemed determined not to leave the girls, said that would mean she could not return until the next day. He said that would do, but Ellen said she could not leave the dinner, as it would spoil. 'Let it spoil,' he said, adding a few choice swear words. He then went out again briefly before returning and demanding that dinner be got ready immediately. The girls returned shortly afterwards.

Minnie told Ellen that her father was very angry, without explaining why, but also asked that dinner be got ready immediately. Dinner was served, but it was not, it seems, a cheerful meal. Ellen heard Prankerd talking loudly and angrily. He was, she said 'a passionate man'. The two older girls went upstairs and their father followed them. He called out: 'Take your hats and go if you don't want any money.' When they returned with their hats they stood at the top of the kitchen stairs, and their father, who had followed them about the house, now demanded to know where they were going. They replied very softly, and he swore at them and said he supposed they were going to his friend John Prankerd. This John Prankerd was a relation, and the remark about him being a friend was made sarcastically – as would later be revealed, the two, though once friends, now very much disliked one another, not least because the girls turned to this relative for help and advice. Both the girls and their father then went into the schoolroom and he locked himself in with them.

Ellen heard him shouting – she called it 'holloaing' – for about ten minutes, and then when the noise subsided, he came out, locking the girls back in and went to his bedroom, saying as he returned and relocked the door, 'Now then, what do you say to this?' To her horror,

The faithful servant Ellen sees Kate escaping over the wall. Bath Central Library

about two minutes later she heard the report of firearms – 'I thought of a pistol': she said. It was fired four times in rapid succession and then there was quiet – no moaning or sound of anyone falling. Ellen went into the passage from the kitchen, which was in the basement, and led to the garden. She saw Kate on the garden wall, bleeding very much. Kate said: 'Go to Minnie.' Courageously, Ellen went upstairs and tried the door of the schoolroom. It was still locked, but when she asked if she could come in she heard only a faint moan. Then she heard 'a very great noise in the throat' which she took to be the master. Ellen decided it was time to seek assistance and went downstairs for her cloak. At the top of the stairs she met Mr Prankerd who looked her very straight in the face before going back and locking himself in the schoolroom. Ellen ran next door to Reverend J H Wray's house, to raise the alarm. Mr Wray's servant told her that Mr Wray had gone for the doctor for Kate, who had got over the wall. The police were also sent for, and Inspector Henry Sutton soon arrived on the scene.

Sutton found an alarmed group of people outside and inside the house. The parlour doors being locked Sutton ordered them to be forced open. Behind it, in a large pool of blood, lay the body of

The angry John Prankerd shoots his eldest daughter. Bath Central Library

Margaret Methuen Prankerd – Minnie. She was quite dead, having been shot twice through the head. A trail of blood marked Kate's incredible escape, for she too had been shot twice through the head, the bullets having entered her mouth. Of Prankerd himself there was no sign, until Sutton went into the front attic. Here, lying on the bed, he found the body of Mr Prankerd. A strong smell of almonds pervaded the air, and his mouth and the eyes were open. Prankerd had taken his own life with prussic acid. There was no doubt that he had made clear preparations to murder the two elder girls. Had Ellen not staunchly refused to go, he would probably have killed the youngest as well – he certainly had the ammunition to do it. It appears he perhaps intended to flee abroad, taking the fifteen year old with him. The pistol had been hidden in a bureau, where it was later discovered. But once Ellen refused to leave the house and then Kate had escaped, he must have known there was no way out.

The question of his sanity was raised. His relative, John Prankerd, thought him mad and, since he was a surgeon, his opinion clearly

It was over the garden wall between Nos 1 and 2 Spencers's Belle Vue that Kate, seriously injured and in a state of shock, made her escape. The author

counted for something. He told the inquest jury more about his namesake. He explained that his grandfather had married twice, he himself being descended from the first wife. The other John Prankerd, now deceased, was aged about forty-six, and was the son of the second wife, but had been born before the marriage. He had known him intimately all his life, but for twenty years the deceased had lived abroad. The previous summer he had spent time with his family at Langport, where the surgeon lived, when he had seemed sound in health and mind. He explained that the previous week he had received a telegram from Minnie, asking him to come to Bath immediately. A second telegram, explaining that her father had used violence against Kate brought him down the next day and he went to friends at No. 23 The Circus, from whence Minnie had sent the telegram. The friend started to tell him something of what was going on, when Prankerd himself came in. At first he seemed friendly, but then became excited and disagreeable in manner, and swore that he would have no interference in his business. He accused his relation of having had his daughters to stay at Christmas just so that he could find out more about him. The surgeon gathered more information about the state of affairs from Ellen while the family were out, and he finally called on the schoolmaster's medical attendant, Dr. Hensley. They went to Spencer's Belle Vue, where Hensley managed to calm the angry father. Hensley promised to keep in touch with the surgeon, explaining that his patient was just excited from a variety of circumstances. The sceptical surgeon personally considered that it was more likely that he was suffering from delirium tremens. He subsequently heard other stories that convinced him his relative was insane. On one occasion, while on holiday in France, he had taken the two older girls out in a boat, then asked them to choose which of three forms of death they would prefer; that he should upset the boat so that they drowned, that he should shoot them or they should take poison. He then made them each drink a half a pint of laudanum, but the rolling of the boat made them vomit. The coroner, however, was clearly unimpressed with the surgeon's opinion, and gave a clear direction to the jury to

Kate escaped with her life but could she ever have recovered from the mental shock of her terrible experience? Bath Central Library

find that the verdict was suicide while in a sound state of mind. It took the jury an hour and a quarter, but they finally followed the coroner's guidance.

Both Minnie and John Prankerd lie buried in Locksbrook cemetery. Her funeral took place by day, and she was buried in a grave with her mother, but the unhappy Mr Prankerd, whose mind seems to have been unhinged by the death of his wife, was buried at night in unconsecrated ground. Kate recovered, and was able to state where the missing sister was. But one wonders if someone whose father has stood over her and calmly shot her twice with the words, 'Will that finish you?' can ever truly recover.

The twentieth Century – the father-in-law who wouldn't die

In our final story in this chapter, it was a father who died. If it had not been for the fact that a helpless and confused old man was done to death, the story would be almost farcical, so inept were the efforts of the murderer, Reginald Ivor Hinks. The story began when, in 1933, Hinks made the acquaintance of Mrs Constance Anne Jeffries, a divorcée with a five-year old daughter, Beryl, who was living with her aged father at No. 43 Milton Avenue, Bath. It later transpired she had three sons by her first husband, but they lived with their father. The houses in Milton Avenue are in a part of Bath known as Poet's Corner, built in the late nineteenth and early twentieth century. Although not one of Bath's top addresses, it is still a desirable place to live. The streets, all named after poets, are tree-lined, and some of the houses are substantial. Mr Pullen, Constance's father, was a retired master tailor from Dorking, where he still had a shop and some cottages. Unfortunately for him, he had become frail and was almost senile. His wife having died early in 1933, his daughter was now caring for him with the aid of two nurses, Mrs Smith during the day and Mr Strange at night. In a very short space of time, Reginald Hinks and Constance Jeffries were married. The new Mrs Hinks appears not to have looked into her husband's life story. It was not a savoury one.

Born in 1900, in Middlesex (although his family lived in South Africa), he went to live with his brothers in Bath when he was seventeen, and gained an apprenticeship at Stothert and Pitts. He did not last long. Not only was his work poor, but workmates became suspicious that he was responsible for the disappearance of their tools. He left before he was sacked, in 1921, and joined the army. There, his record in the Royal Corps of Signals states he was 'slack, lazy and untidy' and he was dismissed. He tried again by joining a fusiliers regiment under the name of Hanks, but was discharged as medically unfit. From then on he drifted from job to job and woman to woman, mainly in the London area. In 1929, while working as a butler, under the name of Reginald Ivor Percival, he was charged with two counts of theft from his employers and their guests. When his then girlfriend received a legacy of £225, Hinks managed to get his hands on it. He subsequently gave her a severe beating and they separated. After a few more years of living like this, he returned to Bath. One of his first acts in the city, on his arrival on Christmas Eve 1932 was to snatch a woman's handbag containing £100. The following year he secured a job as a vacuum cleaner salesman. This is how he met Constance. He discovered that she had £2,000 and her father was also well-to-do. However unpleasant a person Hinks seem to have been, one cannot deny he must also have been remarkably charming, and the two were married after what the paper would later describe as a hurricane courtship. Hinks moved in, later quitting his job. One of his first actions was to persuade Mr Pullen to sell the shop in Dorking for about £900, and to make the money over to him. The solicitor in Dorking only saw Mr and Mrs Hinks, and was totally unaware of Mr Pullen's debility. With the £900 Hinks bought a car and moved the family to a smaller property, a mock-Tudor house called Wallasey in Englishcombe Lane. He then dismissed the nurses, on the grounds that they were spiritualists and were upsetting his wife with their table-turning and knocking on walls, not to mention trying to contact the late Mrs Pullen. He then took over the care of Mr Pullen and put him on a restricted diet, all, he said, in the interests of economy.

Reginald Hinks. Bath Central Library

The cause of this economy was that the family solicitor, Dr Carpenter, alarmed by the way he considered the old man's estate was being dissipated, had achieved an order in lunacy to safeguard Mr Pullen. This prevented Constance Hinks from drawing out the £20 a week she had been removing from her father's savings and from selling the house in Milton Avenue, which had belonged to her mother. In her father's will she would eventually receive all the property but until then the solicitor advised the couple to let Milton Avenue at five guineas a week. Carpenter also made the Dorking solicitor aware of the situation, and the sale of the other Dorking properties was stopped. Until the father died, there would be no more access to money. The eighty-one-year-old, though apparently frail, was clearly as tough as old boots, and Hinks decided his demise would

Pullen's house, No. 43 Milton Avenue, which Constance endeavoured to sell until prevented by her father's solicitor. The author

have to be hastened. Unluckily for him, Pullen was tougher than even Hinks thought, and it took longer than expected.

His first attempt was to send him out alone on walks in the city centre, in the hope he would have an accident. When this failed, he tried a new tactic, which was foiled by a startled local policeman. One night in the autumn of 1933, he saw James Pullen apparently sleep-walking, while being followed at a discreet distance by a car, driven by Reginald Hinks. He was, he said, merely keeping watch on his father-in-law who was engaged in a ten-mile walk. At this point the old man collapsed, and Hinks bundled him into the car and took him home. The next time the police came across James Pullen was when they were called to a disturbance on a bus. There was Mr Pullen, demanding to go to Dorking and offering four matchsticks and a pencil in payment of the fare.

Still the old man survived. Something more lethal was clearly required. On 30 November, at 7.30 in the evening, Hinks called the police, a doctor, and Bath Fire Brigade ambulance, which carried oxygen. His father-in-law had been found unconscious in the bath. The bathing arrangements were slightly odd – Beryl bathed first, and then, while her mother got her supper and put her to bed, her grandfather was allowed to bathe. By the time Mr Pullen got in, it must have been decidedly unpleasant – grubby, soapy and chilly. Hinks explained that he normally watched over him, but he had had to fetch his clean underwear, and on his return found Mr Pullen with his head under water. However, when the emergency services arrived, they found that Pullen had made a remarkable recovery. He was now sitting up in the bath, from which the water had been emptied, wrapped in a blanket and clutching a hot water bottle. If Hinks had thought this shock would kill him, he was wrong. What was more, the doctor remarked that Mr Pullen was in very good health for a man of his years. Perhaps Hinks' exercise regime and strict diet had actually toughened him up!

But Mr Pullen had less than twenty-four hours to enjoy his rude health. The next day the emergency services were once again called to Wallasey. Mrs Hinks had gone to the cinema, leaving Hinks and Beryl with her father. Hinks later called the police to say his father in law had tried to gas himself. The old man had gone to the outside lavatory then come into the kitchen and turned on the gas. When the police came, they found Pullen lying in the kitchen where there was a faint smell of gas. Two coats had been draped over the oven door, shelves had been removed and the dog's blanket had been placed in the oven. Hinks said he had found two gas taps turned on, and had pulled Pullen from the oven. 'You might find a bruise on the back of his head,' he remarked to the police officer who rushed to the aid of the old man. 'I pulled him out of the gas stove and his head fell with a bump on the floor.' An alert police officer thought this was an odd thing to say, and made a note of it. It was to prove a crucial piece of evidence. The unhappy Pullen at this stage was still alive, but this final incident was too much, and he died as respiration was being applied.

The inquest at first attracted little attention – it was just another inquest on a suicide, but when both Mr Pullen's own doctor, Scott Reid, and subsequently the police surgeon, Dr Harper, queried

Elsom for Floral Tributes and Choicest Flowers

THE CONSERVATORIES

The Bath Chronicle and Herald

SATURDAY, JANUARY 20, 1934.

CELLULOID BATHING

ELASTIC BAND

EDWIN HANCOCK

31 Broad Stree

MR. HINKS ARRESTED

Wilful Murder Verdict At Inquest

Jury Deliberate Only 25 Minutes

Amazed Man Exclaims "Whatever For, Sir?"

Sent for Trial on Coroner's Warrant

NINETY FAMILIES BENEFIT

MAYOR'S EMPLOYMENT FUND DOING WELL

NOT A BURGLAR!

GONE OUT OF BUSINESS

Fate of Bath Branch of N.C.U.

BATH FOR A LIFE

TWO OUT OF THRE REACH AGE

DEATHS EXCEED

The inquest became headline news when Hinks was arrested. Bath Central Library

aspects of the alleged suicide, the press and the public became interested. Scott Reid, in particular, stated from the outset that he believed the bruise had been caused by a blow administered before any gas, and was sufficient to stun the old man. Dr Harper confirmed this. It was also suspicious that there was so little smell of gas – there was only a faint odour in the victim's mouth. Meanwhile the funeral had taken place, during which Mrs Hinks had collapsed back into her husband's arms. It was not the first time she would collapse. Matters for Mr and Mrs Hinks were going to get much, much worse. The next Saturday's paper contained a double page spread, and before long it was front-page news. Mrs Hinks was at pains to tell the inquest jury how difficult a man her father had been, at times striking both her and her mother. He had a violent temper and threw things. He was, she declared, suicidal, and had been caught playing with a knife and with the gas fire, which he would poke with pieces of paper. Meanwhile, she declared, her husband was kindness itself to her father. It must be said that both Mrs Smith and Mr Strange, the nurses who had been dismissed by Hinks, corroborated most of this. From time to time throughout her evidence she would break down in tears or collapse, while her husband would rush to bring her glasses of water.

Out of Hinks's own mouth came the lie which was to hang him. The autopsy showed that the bruise had been sustained before Pullen had inhaled the gas. Dr Scott Reid was adamant that in Mr Pullen's confused state he would not have understood the need for coats to hold the gas in the oven. He also considered it was unlikely he could have turned on the taps, despite Mrs Hinks' evidence that her father made himself cups of tea on the stove. The inquest ended sensationally, when the jury gave their verdict as wilful murder by Reginald Ivor Hinks, and before anyone could quite believe what was happening, he was arrested. After the committal proceedings at the Bath magistrates' court, when Mrs Hinks fainted and burst into tears again, her husband was remanded in custody and referred for trial at the Old Bailey.

The result was still not a foregone conclusion. One expert declared that he had conducted tests and believed the bruise on the back of the head was entirely consistent with the head being banged on the floor as Hinks had described. Yet despite this, the verdict went against him. As the prosecuting counsel said, 'This old, tottering man was supposed to have gone upstairs to the bedroom, kissed the little girl asleep, gone downstairs, out of the back door to the lavatory, come back into the kitchen, removed coat and waistcoat, placed a piece of blanket into the stove to make himself happy and comfortable, removed three shelves from the stove, arranged the coat around the oven door, turned on the two taps, removed his slippers, and then laid down with his head in the stove to await his maker – and all this in the space of twenty-five minutes.' It was enough to persuade the jury of nine men and three women. Hinks was found guilty and sentenced to death. Mrs Hinks was led sobbing from the court, while the three women jurors were visibly distressed.

It was now open season on Hinks in the press. Previous women in his life rushed to tell the newspapers what a beast he was. Unknown to Hinks, there was also a warrant out for his arrest for the bag snatching. The victim had recognized his picture in the paper and come forward. Hinks appealed, but to no avail. The judges decided that although the evidence was circumstantial, the likelihood of the senile old man being able to arrange the coats around the stove, put his head inside and then turn on the taps was just too remote. The death sentence remained. Not everyone was happy with this. Hundreds of letters were received begging for his sentence to be commuted to life. They were ignored. On 3 May 1934, Hinks was hanged at Horfield prison, Bristol, still maintaining his innocence. Whatever his faults, he had remained protective of his wife throughout. He had begged some facts to be kept from her. 'She is only a little thing, and like her father, very mental,' he remarked to one official. Throughout his trials he was sustained by her presence. He told the prison governor that he preferred death to life imprisonment, so that Constance could start life again.

He hoped she would marry again, so that there would be someone to look after her. But was she the weak little figure that everyone thought?

By 1930 Constance was divorced from her first husband, a very unusual thing in those days, and showing a marked independence of mind. She drove a car, again not something many women did then. And she seems happily to have given her consent to Hinks's treatment of her father and colluded in his attempt to get his hands on her father's money. She had insisted during the trial that her father often fell, and that he was suicidal, yet at no time had she reported this to his doctor. And, although she professed to be upset by her father's death, she was much more concerned by the fate of her husband, her father's murderer. Or was she? No one seems to have asked themselves just how involved she was in the murder, and whether perhaps Hinks was a willing dupe. No one, that is, except a reporter on the *Bath Chronicle and Herald*. He, it seems, had been keeping a watch on Mrs Hinks and on the day before the execution he was rewarded by seeing a trim figure smartly dressed in a grey coat and hat drive up in a large car and enter her solicitors' offices on North Parade. It was Mrs Hinks. After an hour and a half she came out, causing a slight sensation as she drove through town because in the car, on the back seat, was her pet marmoset. It was hardly the act of a woman trying to avoid notice. The reporter drove after her and at Twerton tried to persuade her to stop. But, giving him a little smile, she drove confidently away. 'Mrs Hinks appeared,' he wrote acidly in the paper, 'to have recovered her composure which was so severely shattered in the Court of Criminal Appeal on Tuesday.' She was now free of every encumbrance – no senile father, no unsatisfactory husbands. She had her hands on all the money and had successfully sold Wallasey to a police officer. She said she was going with Beryl to the South Coast to recuperate, and that is the last we hear of Constance Hinks. Could it just be that this might have been one of those instances where the female was deadlier than male? In the next chapter we consider a case where this was indeed the case.

Chapter 6

Deadlier than the Male

Charlotte Harris and the Bath Poisoning Case

Are women less likely to commit a crime than men? Probably not, but throughout the centuries there seems to have been a sense that this should be the case. Newspapers reported women's crime with a greater sense of shock than if the same crime were committed by a man. It is true that women used different tactics, and came up with different excuses from men, sometimes with comical results. In July 1846 Hannah Pearce was summoned for assaulting Louisa Wickham by throwing water over her in Grove Street. The assault was admitted by the defendant, but in mitigation she pointed out that the water was clean. The magistrates told her this did not excuse the act and fined her 10 shillings and costs or in default fourteen days in prison.

Prostitutes were frequently arrested for a variety of crimes besides prostitution and soliciting. They stole from gullible would-be customers, who seemed to carry astonishingly large amounts of money around with them. A married farmer who went to Bristol Fair 'got among a room full of prostitutes at a public house, who eased him of 109 guineas'. He was carrying around in cash what in modern terms would be about £8,000. The girls must have thought Christmas had come. Smaller sums were equally likely to disappear. In 1850, Fanny Hooper was charged with having stolen Henry Silver's purse. Silver said he met the prisoner in Westgate Street at 8.30 pm one Saturday, and went into a pub with her to have something to drink. This was frequently an introductory move by prostitutes, presumably to make sure a potential client had some cash. They then went to the *King's Head*, in Lilliput Alley, part of which is now one of Bath's best-known French restaurants but was then, to put it bluntly, a knocking-shop. Here, Silver paid for a room and some more drink with half a sovereign, adding the change to the 11 shillings already in his purse. An hour later, Fanny got up and dressed, and left the room. When she did not return, he looked in his pockets and found she had taken all his money except for half a crown. The case was dismissed for lack of evidence, leaving Mr Silver looking rather silly.

Although the King's Head *had ceased to be a pub by the time this picture was taken, it must have looked very similar when aptly named Mr Silver was robbed of his cash by Fanny Hooper.* Author's collection

Usually, the magistrates came down like a ton of bricks on what the paper chose to call 'the frail sisterhood', either locking them up or ordering them to leave the city. The frail sisterhood's antics could sometimes be amusing if they had had too much too drink. Instead of smashing windows or indulging in mindless violence, Louisa Hulbert and another girl 'well known as common prostitutes and night walkers' had entertained themselves after a night on the town by making a disturbance and removing the hats of passers-by. Since they were in the vicinity of the theatre, it may be assumed that some of the passers-by were quite well-to–do and hence not amused at all, even if the girls and the admiring crowd were.

Some women criminals in the eighteenth century found it was beneficial to adopt men's dress. Most notorious of these was Mary Hamilton. In 1746, she was brought to trial for illegally marrying another woman, who was quite unaware of her 'husband's' true sex. Mary was born in Somerset but brought up in Scotland. At the age of fourteen she donned her brother's clothes and headed south. She worked for a quack doctor or two, before becoming one herself. Continuing southwards, she finally ended up back in Somerset, still dressed as a man and known as Charles Hamilton. Arriving in the city of Wells, and finding lodgings in the house of Mrs Creed, she wooed and married Mary Price, Mrs Creed's niece. The record of the wedding is in the parish registers at St Cuthbert's. She fooled her 'wife' by using a dildo to simulate normal sexual relations. Eventually the shocked Mary Price discovered the truth and 'Charles' was revealed to be Mary. She was tried at Taunton Assizes under a clause of the vagrancy act, 'for having by false and deceitful practices endeavoured to impose on some of his Majesty's subjects'. The scandalized county felt justice was served when she was whipped in four market towns and imprisoned for six months.

When it came to murder, however, poison was generally regarded as being a woman's favourite weapon. There were plenty to choose from. In the eighteenth century, cosmetics were a lethal concoction of substances such as white and red lead, mercuric sulphide and arsenic. Right up to Victorian times, ladies would whiten their hands by using small amounts of arsenic. By swallowing very small doses of arsenic they could produce a pale and interesting complexion – it also meant they developed a certain immunity to it, so they could eat or drink food laced with it with impunity while another person would die. There seems little doubt that this technique was sometimes used to dispose of unwanted husbands or lovers. In 1849 the *Bath Chronicle* deplored the increase in the number of poisonings, due to a particularly notorious case.

In August 1849, Bath was shocked to learn that a newly-married lady, Charlotte Harris, was accused of having made herself legally available for the ceremony by poisoning her previous husband. Charlotte Marchant, as she was before her second marriage, lived at Angel Terrace on the Lower Bristol Road. Despite its name, it was not a very heavenly place to live. It was jammed between the newly completed Great Western Railway and the river. In times of heavy rain, Mrs Marchant, her husband Henry and their child would have been one of the many families affected as the river flooded. Today, only one house of the terrace remains, the rest having been pulled down in the 1960s. Charlotte also had a sister in Shepton Mallet, whom she described as being very well off, and a good friend to her.

Early in 1849, Charlotte made friends with Mr William Harris, a man much older than herself. She was thirty-two, he was seventy. He lived in Brookleaze Buildings in Larkhall. Although larger now than it was in 1849, Larkhall still has a village atmosphere. In 1849 it was quite out in the country. Charlotte's husband was a stonemason, who, according to her, was often drunk – Mr Harris, despite or perhaps because of, his years, must have seemed an attractive prospect, especially as he lived in rural Larkhall.

Charlotte was first seen with William Harris early in March. On 22 March they were at the *Larkhall Inn*, and later had dinner at his house, spending several hours together. Over the next week, they began talking of marriage. She assured William Harris that she was

In the foreground can be seen the area where Charlotte lived with her then husband Henry Marchant. In the distance, over to the right, can be the seen the much pleasanter countryside around Larkhall, to which she planned to escape. Author's collection

The Larkhall Inn *has changed little from the days when Charlotte met William Harris there.* Andrew Swift

free of any encumbrances. On Saturday 31 March she decided to make that statement a true one.

Her husband returned to Angel Place at midnight after a night out with his friends – he was, they later said, in good health. His wife gave him some tea. By the next day, he was very ill, and although he went to work on Monday, he was so poorly his workmates persuaded him to return home. On Tuesday, a neighbour, Mary Ann Harvey, asked Charlotte why she did not call the doctor. Charlotte replied that her husband did not want him, and would stab him if he came, but she was finally persuaded to go and find Mr Lloyd, the parish surgeon for Lyncombe and Widcombe. He was out, but Charlotte left a message – with the wrong address. She then went to Larkhall, where she told Hannah Shayler, who cooked for William Harris, that her sister was gravely ill at her house, and she could not stay long. She returned home in time to admit Mr Lloyd, who had finally tracked down where Henry Marchant lived. He believed he was suffering from a severe gastric complaint, and left a bottle of medicine.

During the next few days, Charlotte cared for her husband assiduously, although Mary Harvey asked why she had not given him the medicine. First of all she said she did not believe that Mr Lloyd really knew what was wrong with him. Then she added that as he kept being sick, there was no point in giving medicine because he would

All that remains today of Angel Place is one house. The author

not keep it down. Lloyd also said that Marchant seemed to be better on Thursday, but she did not think he was. Significantly, she was seen giving her husband a bowl of gruel that day. If Marchant really was improving, it must have given Charlotte a nasty moment. During this time she was not seen at Larkhall. Marchant finally died on Easter Saturday, 7 April, a week after he had been taken ill. The following day, Charlotte dressed herself, not in mourning but in coloured clothes, to the dismay of the neighbours. When challenged, she said she was going to stay with her uncle in Walcot. She was actually off

Brookleaze Buildings, where William Harris lived. The author

to see William Harris. She warned Hannah Shayler that she would probably hear that her husband was dead. 'But I thought you did not have a husband,' said a surprised Hannah. Charlotte said that she had, but he had now died and he was such a drunkard that the neighbours said, 'she ought to be down on her knees to think he was dead'.

Marchant's funeral was on Friday 13 April. Hannah's husband, Daniel, attended with Charlotte, later spending an hour at her house. Charlotte asked if he had a message from Harris. He said he had not, but returned later with a request from Harris to know which parish Charlotte lived in. As she was unable to read and write, Shayler had to put her answer down on paper himself, before taking it back to Harris. The information was needed because Harris was getting a marriage licence.

On Saturday, Charlotte and Hannah went shopping for items that Charlotte would need at Larkhall, and in the evening the Shaylers began helping to move her belongings over to Brookleaze Buildings. At 4.00 am on Monday, Daniel Shayler took the last of Charlotte Marchant's belongings to No. 15 Brookleaze Buildings. Later that day, at St Saviour's Church, Larkhall, Charlotte became Mrs Harris. Her husband had been dead just nine days.

No. 15 Brookleaze Buildings, where Charlotte had hoped to make a new start in life, is the house in the middle of this picture. The author

If Charlotte thought that by moving across town, the good people of Angel Place would not find out, she was wrong. Even today, Bath is a village as far as gossip is concerned. It was far more so then. Her scandalized neighbours soon started talking, and finally drew the attention of the authorities to this rather speedy marriage. The body was exhumed and, despite Charlotte's protestations that she did not want her husband 'cut up', there was an autopsy. A large quantity of arsenic was found in the body. It was this inescapable fact that Charlotte's lawyer could not explain away, although some of the evidence, including the medical evidence, was contradictory. One witness said Charlotte had asked her to buy two pennyworth of arsenic. Another said she had seen Charlotte, in Mr Bright's chemist's shop in Southgate Street, buying the arsenic herself. Her evidence was very specific. She had heard the prisoner tell Mr Bright that she needed it to kill the rats which came up from the river. Unfortunately for the witness, this evidence was contradicted by the chemist himself who said he did not remember the event, and in this he was supported by another customer, Mr Sendall. Yet another witness was forced to admit that, having said he had seen the prisoner in the shop, he had not, in fact, seen her face. And all this happened at a time when Hannah Shayler had said she was at Larkhall. Bright's assistant, however, recalled that he had seen the prisoner in the shop, but he did not remember when.

On the medical side, it was pointed out by Mr Saunders, for the defence, that the usual symptom of arsenic poisoning was diarrhoea, while Mr Lloyd had admitted that Marchant was constipated. Yet nothing could explain away the fact that on 31 March Henry Marchant was in good health, on 7 April he was dead, the only person who had given him food was his wife, and arsenic was in the body. Despite Mr Saunders suggesting that Marchant might have administered it to himself, the jury was not convinced. After a careful summing up by the judge, Mr Justice Cresswell, they withdrew, and after an hour returned a guilty verdict. The judge donned his black cap and pronounced the death sentence. She was to hang. It could have been worse. Less than a hundred years before, a nineteen-year-old woman, Susannah Bruford, had been burnt at the stake at Wells for poisoning her husband, a form of execution which had only been abolished in 1790. And at this point, the distraught Charlotte Harris played her trump card. Her defence counsel rose to his feet and declared that she was with child. This caused the proverbial sensation in the court. After a consultation between the assize judges, the lawyers and the High Sherriff, the court was declared closed, and the Sheriff was empowered to collect a panel of twelve people to decide if this were true. Obviously, the panel had to be of women, and there was pandemonium as women, of which there a great number in the room, tried by any means to avoid being chosen. At last twelve were selected, and declined the offer of a medical man's assistance. After a very short time, they returned, confirming that she was indeed with child. Charlotte, who had fainted several times during the trial, fainted again, and was removed from the court 'in a very pitiable condition'.

Charlotte Harris escaped the hangman. In November, her death sentence was rescinded 'until further notice' and she does not appear on any list of those subsequently executed. Her undue haste in getting remarried had been her downfall. If she had waited for a reasonable time, she would have got away with it. Perhaps she really did love William Harris and wanted to be with him – perhaps she felt if she waited too long he might die and her chance of a new life would be gone forever.

The moral of this story for would-be husband poisoners seems to be: don't upset the neighbours.

CHAPTER 7

No Way to Treat the Lower Orders

Three tales of treatment meted out to those in lower orders, and of the different outcomes

Justice in eighteenth-century Bath could be curiously inconsistent. In this chapter we look at three cases of neglect and cruelty meted out by those who should have known better to those in their care. Yet the man in the worst case got off scot free, while one man who had tried to his best for the victim ended up being accused of his death.

The cook who was hit with a scrubbing brush

In March 1782, an inquest was called to enquire into the death of a servant, Ann Allen, at a house in Monmouth Street. As the inquest went on, and witnesses were called, a story of incredible ill treatment and neglect began to unfold.

Ann Allen had been servant to Mr and Mrs Chitchester, who lived in Belmont Row, an elegant terrace on the slopes of Lansdown. Ann had been a servant there for some time and was employed to dress – or prepare – the dinner. Mary Ham, who had been a servant at the Chitchesters' for about three months, had noticed that Mrs Chitchester harried and scolded Ann Allen but did not strike her. It was, however, a rather different story with Henry Chitchester. Mary said that he attended while Ann was preparing the dinner and struck her about the head if it was not ready in time. Mary Ham did not believe that Ann Allen received any injury to her person from these blows, but admitted that Ann was weak and had a poor constitution. She had also noticed that her legs had some wounds on them. Ann Rouzel, another servant, said that she had seen Henry Chitchester pull Ann Allen by the ear and slap the side of her face 'but not to hurt her.' However, she had told Ann Rouzel that five weeks previously he had hit her on the arm with a scrubbing brush.

Not surprisingly, the Chitchesters did not seem to keep servants very long, and the next witness was William Chapman, who had been

Mr and Mrs Chitchester lived near the top of this elegant terrace. The author

a servant but left three weeks before. He had seen Henry hit Ann Allen about the head and two weeks before he left he had seen her injured when she had been struck on the right arm and in the side.

It appears that the unhappy cook's state of health was becoming an embarrassment, and it was decided to remove her from the house. Mrs Chitchester called Charles Green, an apothecary and asked if he thought her servant had smallpox. No, he said, it was a putrid fever. Ann Allen was then bundled into a sedan chair, wrapped only in a blanket, and taken to Mrs Halfpenny's in Monmouth Row. The two sedan chairmen, John Gardner and Daniel Alexander, were unhappy about this. First they thought their passenger had smallpox, so understandably they were unwilling to take her. Then some person in the passage at Belmont said it was something worse. The two men, satisfied that it was nothing catching, said they thought it was a shame to carry the woman out of the house being so ill, but, reluctantly, they did so.

Sarah Jones, who had been a servant with the Chitchesters for a very short time, had been sent to find lodgings for Ann Allen. Ann had told her that she had been ill treated, and Sarah had told Mrs Halfpenny. After the incident with the scrubbing brush the cook had

Ill as Ann Allen was, she was bundled into a sedan chair and carried down this steep hill and across town to a lodging house. The author

been unable to rise out of her chair for some time. Ann had told Sarah she was sorry that she, Sarah, had gone to live at Belmont, for it was an unhappy place.

Elizabeth Halfpenny was then called. She had been summoned to Mrs Chitchester, who had told her she had an apprentice girl she feared had smallpox. Mrs Halfpenny could see that Ann was very ill and in a shaky condition, her lips and tongue very white. By the time she arrived at the house in Monmouth Street she was weak and languid and she died the next day. Her legs were sore and smelt offensive. When Mrs Chitchester was told, she ordered Mrs Halfpenny to have her buried soon, which was done on the Thursday, in Walcot churchyard.

Neither of the Chitchesters was called. Henry, perhaps wisely, had left Bath and gone to his country house at Ivelchester – or Ilchester, as we now call it. He need not have worried. He was a man of some substance and influence in Bath and it showed. The body had been handed over to three surgeons who conducted a post-mortem. One must remember that surgeons then did not enjoy the prestige they do now, although their status was improving, and these three certainly seem to have been influenced by someone. During the post- mortem, they said, they found no sign of violence upon her. For some time before her death she had been ailing, and infirm and afflicted with a putrid fever. She died, they said, in a natural way. No remarks of censure were made against Mr Henry Chitchester, whose vile treatment of his cook must have hastened her end, even if it had not directly caused it.

The starving lodger

Elizabeth Greenwood was a lodging-house-keeper at No. 4 Orange Grove, but if her treatment of Ann Ames was typical, it was a lodging-house to avoid. Witnesses reported that Ann had been left in a cold room in her bed gown and shift. For breakfast she was given two half

No. 4 Orange Grove today. The author

rounds of bread and butter and a cup of tea. Her dinner consisted of two or three potatoes, sometimes meat and cabbage, but no bread. Tea was the same as breakfast. She was given no water, although she said she was thirsty. The servant had protested about the treatment but Elizabeth Greenwood had said she was flighty. Elizabeth herself denied this. She said that Ann Ames had not paid her in money, although she had taken her lodger's furniture as rent, the value amounting to between £20 and £65. She said that Ann Ames had been with her for over three years, and had had three good meals a day. Another witness, however, denied this, and said she had only been there a few months. Ann Fryer told the inquest that she had told Elizabeth that her lodger had been sent to the Bedlam Hospital, but Elizabeth said she had to be kept in her room because she did not want her mixing with the other lodgers.

Unlike Henry Chitchester, Elizabeth Greenwood was not rich and powerful. The inquest verdict was that Ann Ames had died of neglect, cold and lack of food. Mrs Greenwood was not, however, prosecuted.

The soldier's fatal punishment

Our final account is the story of a soldier who had been punished for going AWOL. It throws up a strange paradox of the eighteenth century – that punishments might be so brutal that they were obviously life threatening, but if the recipient did die, someone would have to be punished in their turn. That someone was usually the man at the bottom of the social pile, and so it proved in this case.

James Clarke was an unsatisfactory soldier – there seems little doubt of that. Finally, he decided to quit the army life, which he did by absconding. Recaptured, he was sentenced to 800 lashes. Present at the punishment was Lieutenant Jacob Bryant, adjutant of the 83rd Regiment of Foot. Throughout his evidence, one can almost hear him thinking that the inquest is a great fuss about nothing. He reported that after 175 lashes had been administered on Clarke's naked back with the cat-o'-nine tails in the usual way, it was decided to stop. Godfrey Magerey, the regimental surgeon had dressed his back and left him in the guard house in the parish of St James', where the troops were billeted at the time. The lieutenant had been to see Clarke once or twice everyday. He did not complain about his whipping, said the lieutenant, and appeared strong and, in the adjutant's view, could have borne a larger number of lashes. Bryant did not observe that anything was wrong until the Saturday when the lips appeared white, at which point he called the surgeon.

Godfrey Magerey then took the witness box. He had seen the punishment, and said that Clarke was not exhausted after it. He dressed his back and went to see the soldier daily, dressing the back when necessary and saw no material change until 5.00 pm on the Saturday. He then saw that he was under 'an acute case of inflammatory fever' with a high pulse. He was trying to vomit, so Margerey gave him an emetic. He then did not see him again until 10.00 pm on Sunday, when he found him delirious and dying.

Doubtless the army would have swept all this under the carpet had it not been for the churchwardens of St James's parish, who probably resented the army being billeted there. They saw the body and called in Nicholas Kelly to take a look. He rather concurred with the army surgeon. In his view, from the appearance of the back he felt the punishment was not extreme but rather a mild one. The skin was not lacerated, 'which is usual in extreme punishment of this kind'. William Day, the surgeon who conducted the post-mortem, did not agree, however. He saw clear marks of putrefaction in the back and in

The statue of Justice on Bath's Guildhall is not blindfolded – the treatment meted out to Mr Margerey was certainly very different from that received by the much richer, more gentlemanly, Mr Chitchester. Andrew Swift

his view Clarke had died in consequence of the punishment. He also complained that it had been too long before he had seen the body.

The inquest jury agreed with Day. They held that James Clarke had 'laboured and languished under a grievous disease of body, to wit fever, produced through the legal punishment inflicted upon him'. The fever increasing, he died. The jury then added that it was 'through the neglect of Godfrey Magerey, the surgeon, in not giving him medical assistance and not by any other means'. This seems manifestly unfair. Poor Godfrey Magerey had done his best for Clarke, dressing his back so carefully that the normal marks did not appear. Yes, he left a sick man for over twenty-four hours, but it is quite clear that he was on call. Why did no one tell him that he should make an urgent visit? And why had the affair caused such an outrage in the city that the Mayor conducted the investigation? We cannot be sure, but one gets the feeling that there was tension between the army and the civilian population. So when a chance came to strike at the army, the council took it. It stopped short of blaming the officer, who might have had powerful connections, so poor Godfrey Magerey became the scapegoat. Yet compared with Henry Chitchester he had been a veritable Good Samaritan. No wonder the statue of Justice over the Guildhall in Bath has no blindfold – she was clearly expected to judge the social standing of those who came before her.

Chapter 8

Fighting Fair and Square

The dubious morality of duelling

The image we have of the past is coloured by the impressions we get from books and portraits of the time as well as modern films and romantic fiction. In the latter, even violence is often romanticized. It is easy to forget just how violent the past was, and how ready people were to turn to sticks, swords and pistols to settle quite minor disputes. Duelling was a formalized version of this violence, with its own rules and morality. Even the law was in doubt – when someone died his opponent was sometimes charged with murder, but frequently pleaded successfully that it was self-defence or manslaughter. As we shall see, the working classes also saw the duel as a perfectly reasonable method of sorting out a problem, although the law tended to look on fatal outcomes of these duels with more severity. Richard Beau Nash was not one of the first to see that duelling was undesirable – Parliament, prompted by Queen Anne, had tried and failed to bring in an act banning it in 1713. Nash, however, succeeded in stamping out the practice in Bath, at least within the city boundary. Nash became Master of Ceremonies when the previous incumbent was killed in a duel about a game of cards. He well knew that many duels, even when conducted with seconds and observers, ended as unseemly stabbing matches, with the protagonists scrambling on the ground, after pistols failed or swords snapped. Yet despite all he and the law could do, duels, conducted in secret, continued.

Perhaps the best-known duel in Bath was the second of the two fought between the playwright Richard Sheridan and another suitor for the hand of the beautiful, talented singer Elizabeth Linley. Sheridan had already escorted Elizabeth to France in March 1772 to help her avoid the attentions of this man, Major Thomas Mathews, and the gossips suggested that the two had gone through a form of marriage whilst there. Mathews, incensed at being cheated of his prize, put insulting comments about his rival into the Bath newspapers. Far from persuading Bath that he was a wronged man, public opinion swung even further behind Sheridan, especially as Mathews was rumoured to be married, and Mathews retreated to London.

Beau Nash stopped duelling inside the city – but it still went on outside the walls.
Andrew Swift

Here he fought a duel with Sheridan which he lost when Sheridan seized his sword, and he was forced to beg for his life. Undaunted, he persisted with his allegations, and Sheridan and he fought a return match on Kingsdown, a hill to the east of Bath. Sheridan tried his earlier tactic of rushing Mathews, but this time the Major was ready for him. In the struggle, the two men fell, and their swords were broken. Mathews managed to get on top, and picking up what remained of his sword, demanded that Sheridan yield. He refused, and Mathews then began stabbing him with the broken blade. Rather belatedly the seconds rushed in, and Mathews went off in a coach while Sheridan, badly injured was taken home to receive medical attention. The result was quite the reverse of what Mathews had been

Richard Sheridan. Author's collection

seeking, however, for now Elizabeth Linley openly declared her love for Sheridan.

Mathews seems to have been notorious for fighting – one reason that Elizabeth Linley had put up with his pleas, threats and insinuations for so long was that she feared that if her father knew, he would feel impelled to challenge him, at the risk of his life. Although Mathews made a third attempt to provoke Sheridan into a duel, the young man was dissuaded by his friends from falling into the trap. Instead he used his experiences in his first play, *The Rivals*, which is set in Bath. Although not an instant success, it became and remains one of theatre's best-loved comedies.

The Linleys had been living in the Royal Crescent when all this took place. Another duel which began with an incident in Royal Crescent was that of Count Rice and Vicomte du Barry. Quite what the trouble was is unclear. The two were reputedly running a gambling hall in Bath's most fashionable address, and this may have been at the root of the problem. Alternatively, it may have been a simple case of jealousy.

Elizabeth Linley gazes out of the portrait while her sister Mary smiles at the artist, Thomas Gainsborough. Author's collection

The two rivals had arrived in Bath from Spa, the great continental watering hole, in 1778. Count James Louis Rice was an Irish soldier of fortune and a friend of Joseph II of Austria, Marie Antoinette's brother. He was also a noted duellist. Vicomte Adolphe du Barry was the son of Comte Jean du Barry, known as Le Roué, who had married off his mistress Jeanne to his brother Guillaume so that they could gain influence with King Louis XV. In this they were spectacularly successful. Madame du Barry, as Jeanne was now called, became the

Royal Crescent, at the bottom of this picture looks peaceful on its hillside setting, but events here in the past provoked our first two duels. The author

King's favourite mistress. She secured Adolphe the position of page at court, and he subsequently married a beautiful young woman, Rose Marie Helene de Tournon, younger cousin of the Prince de Soubise. She had been abducted from a convent by her cousin for this marriage, outraging French society. This, together with the fact that he seemed to be in some financial difficulties is doubtless why he ended up running what seems to have been an illegal casino in the Royal Crescent.

Some accounts say that they fell out over the spoils of a gambling game, involving another resident of the Crescent, Colonel Champion, whom they had relieved of over £600 – about £60,000 in today's terms. But another account says that the viscount had been jealous of Count Rice's attentions to his wife. Du Barry had been in the habit of making offensive remarks about her, and Rice had remonstrated with him, objecting to these imprecations. This was enough for du Barry, who decided that Rice had designs on her, and an argument broke out, which ended in Rice challenging du Barry to a duel. Given Rice's experience and reputation, it was unwise of du Barry to accept.

Seconds and a surgeon were sent for, and shortly after midnight they set out for Claverton Down, where the race course then was. At daybreak the seconds marked out twenty-five yards, and armed each

Royal Crescent at night – this was how Du Barry would have seen it for the last time, as he left for Claverton Down. Andrew Swift

combatant with two pistols and a sword. Pistols of the time were quite likely not to fire properly, one reason being that the powder would flare up in the pan without firing the shot – the origin of the phrase 'flash in the pan'. The agreement was that the conqueror could kill his opponent, even if he was on the ground. The viscount fired first, hitting Count Rice in the thigh, but he, nothing daunted, fired back, hitting du Barry in the chest. Both fired again, without effect, but as they drew their swords and prepared to advance upon each other, Vicomte du Barry staggered and fell. He begged for his life, but barely had Rice agreed to grant it when the viscount groaned, vomited up blood and died. Rice, badly wounded, was hurried back to his lodgings, where he lay several weeks in a dangerous state before recovering. Du Barry's wife was hurried out of the country by a friendly English clergyman before the inquest, where the coroner's jury returned a verdict of manslaughter. Despite this, Rice was indicted for murder, but after explaining the circumstances of the duel, including the fact that he feared that du Barry's jealousy meant that he was planning to poison him, the jury returned a verdict of manslaughter. He escaped with a nominal punishment and went abroad. He could never resist danger, however. It is believed that he was associated with a last ditch efforts to rescue Marie Antoinette from her incarceration, without success. Like Marie Antoinette and Madame du Barry, Vicomte du Barry's father also went to the guillotine, but Vicomte Adolphe du Barry lies buried in the quiet churchyard at Bathampton. The plain gravestone, its wording worn and indistinct, lies almost hidden in a shady corner – a forgotten relic of the violence of the eighteenth century.

Du Barre's Grave at Bathampton. The author

Further down the social scale, duels were more rough and ready affairs – but they were still often fatal. In 1817 John Brown died after he was challenged to a fight because he was working at lower rates than other workers, and hence getting more work. The fight, which took place in Kingsmead Fields, was a proper bare-knuckle fight, with timed rounds. After several rounds Brown tripped and fell into a pit containing stones and broken bottles. At the time no one seems to have taken much notice of this, and he fought four or five more rounds. He was then short of breath, so everyone shook hands and went and had a drink together. Later on he was found dead, but was judged to have died from the fall, not the fight. In 1822, what sounds like a street brawl involving seven men was not deemed to be a fair fight because there were no seconds. Again one of the protagonists, John Fletcher, fell, this time as a result of a blow to the ribs, and later died. On this occasion, his opponent, a man named Denmark, was considered to have committed manslaughter, even though he pointed out that it was Fletcher who wanted to fight. But perhaps the saddest story of all is that of Samuel White, Bath's most reluctant duellist, who was bullied, against his friends' advice, into a bare-knuckle fight

Both John Brown and Samuel White received challenges in a pub called the French Horn. *No picture appears to exist, but it is marked 40 on this map from* The Lost Pubs of Bath. Author's collection

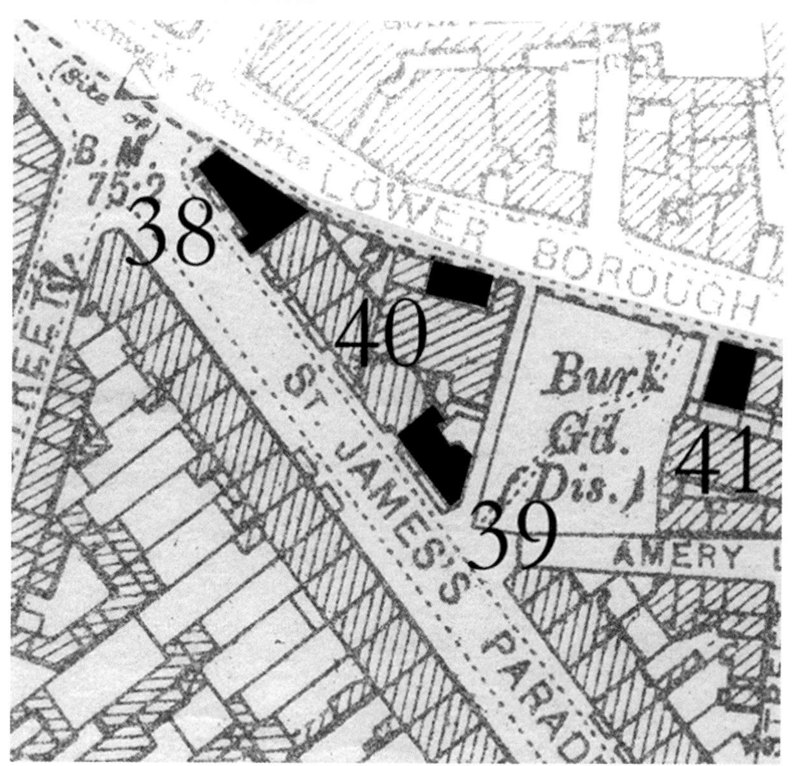

with a belligerent and persistent opponent, Will Davies. It proved to be a fatal decision. And throughout the story, we never know why Samuel White was being pursued so relentlessly by Davies.

The first we hear of Samuel White is on 7 August 1817, in a long vanished pub called the *French Horn*, in the lower part of the town. It was a fairly rough place, and featured frequently in coroner's reports as a place where fights broke out. While drinking there, White was challenged to a fight by a man called Will Davies. His friends persuaded him against it for he had a responsible job as a sedan chairman at the General Hospital, and if the authorities heard that he had been fighting, he might lose his job. White remarked gloomily that he thought Davies would knock him down in the street if he did not fight. Later that evening, when White and a friend called Sam Lewis were passing another pub, the *Pack Horse*, in Widcombe, Davies came out and challenged him again. They arranged to fight at Lansdown Fair. There were boxing booths at this fair, and it seems that this way they hoped to legitimize the fight. White remarked to Lewis that Davies wouldn't let him alone.

The day of Lansdown Fair, 11 August, was wet. White went to the fair with another friend, John Day. It was he who persuaded White that, given the weather, they should call off the fight, and, after having had a beer, they looked for Davies. When Davies heard what they had to say, he suddenly struck the totally unprepared White with two blows to the head and several blows to the chest. At this point White decided there was only one way to end this persecution and that was to stand up and fight, even though the unexpected blow to his head had already caused one eye to go black. They fought several rounds, and the fight was declared in White's favour. Both men, observed one eyewitness, appeared 'much beaten'. White went to the pub on the down and had a glass of rum before riding home on a horse seated behind his mother. His left eye was now very black, and he was much beaten around the left side of the head.

The next day, William Long, surgeon, was called to a house in Chapel Court, where he found the body of Samuel White. It was the classic boxing fatal injury – a haemorrhage inside the skull on the left side. Davies was later charged with felony and manslaughter. Nothing sums up the futility of duelling as much as this sad little story. White, who had never wanted to fight in the first place, had won the battle but lost his life.

CHAPTER 9

The Mind Unbalanced

Some sad tales of those who died while the balance of their mind was disturbed

Violent death is always shocking, but suicide carries with it a peculiar horror, especially for the relatives left behind. Although decriminalised in 1961, the act of taking one's own life can be a particularly cruel way of inflicting pain on others. Today, a coroner's verdict suggests that anyone killing themselves does so 'whilst the balance of the mind was disturbed'. This, with its implications that it was a moment of madness, may help the relatives a little. Alternatively, a possible suicide may be passed off as an accident. Sometimes, of course, there is genuine doubt, but on other occasions, one must assume that the feelings of the family were being taken into consideration. Unfortunately, it can leave the case so unresolved that it is almost more distressing. Faced with a suicide, most of us can only ask the question – what unbalances the mind of an individual so much that he or she decides to take that ultimate step from life into the unknowable world of death?

To take that step, many have resorted to extraordinary lengths – others took easy ways out. In the days before safety razors, the temptation for a man to cut his throat in times of trouble was all too easy. Others hanged themselves, with a variety of cords including, in one case in Bath, a black silk handkerchief, while others took the dreadful route of arsenic. And when all other methods failed, there was always the river. For anyone bent on self-destruction, the deep and swiftly flowing Avon, which snakes its way around Bath, was a fairly certain way out of this world.

In times gone by, when poverty was grinding, even in the elegant city of Bath, when there were no counsellors or pills to help with depression, when alcohol and opium were the only pain-killers, the coroners' reports contain the sorry records of many who voluntarily gave up on life's struggle. Or did they? In two of the three cases detailed below, the inquest jury decided they were accidents. One of those decisions seems to fly in the face of the evidence. The other remains an unresolved mystery to this day.

The sad life of Fanny Dayer

Our first case dates from 1816, and through it we learn more about one of Bath's industries that was rarely mentioned in the guidebooks. It was prostitution. Reverend John Skinner of Camerton implored his parishioners not to let their daughters work in service in Bath. He knew all too well that many would end up out of a job, often in deep trouble, and finally fall into the clutches of the brothel-keepers, particularly in the notorious Avon and Corn Street area. One of the few books that does mention prostitutes, Pierce Egan's *Walks Through*

The Avon Street area of Bath in the late Georgian period. It changed little until the 1960 clearances. Author's collection

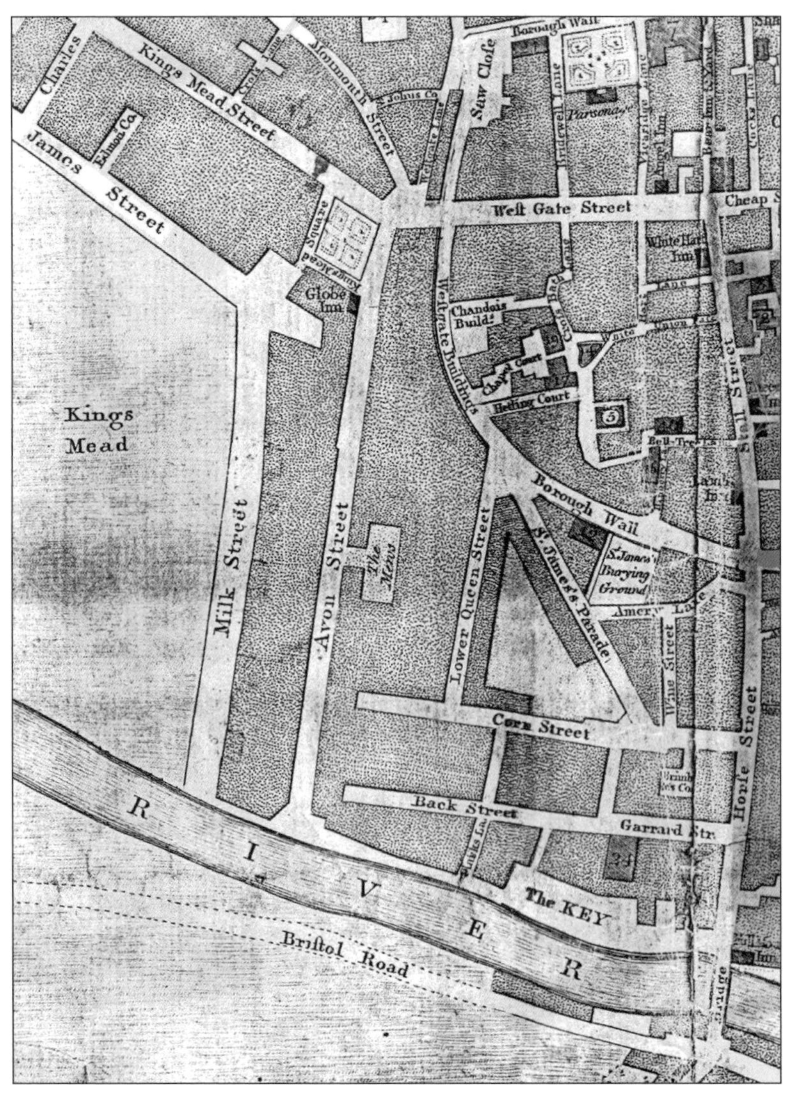

Bath (1819), refers to the girls jocularly as 'the nymphs of Avon Street'. The truth, as we shall see, was much grimmer. This is the sad story of Francis Dayer.

Fanny, as she was known, seems to have come from a respectable family. The cause of her leaving home was the old, old tale we still hear today – she was a teenager who had decided to go her own way, to the anger of her parents. Her mother testified that it was due to her misconduct that she had not lived with her family for about eight months, during which time they had heard nothing from her. By February 1816, she seems to have been well known in Avon Street, although it appears she did not have permanent lodgings there. Another girl, Hester Dully, who did, said that Fanny had been sleeping at No. 26 Avon Street, for several nights. On Saturday 24 February, about 7.00 pm Fanny came in with a young man and asked if they could sleep there. Hester showed them a room upstairs. You cannot help but feel sorry for the young man, whose name was David Price. It turned out to be not quite the jolly evening he was expecting. He had known Fanny for a couple of months, and they had met that night in the kitchen of the *Ship and Nelson*, a pub in Southgate Street, a busy but far from fashionable street not far away. There, Fanny drank two glasses of rum, a gin and part of a quart of beer. She was, he admitted 'much in liquor'. They then agreed to sleep together.

Fanny was, apparently, already in an unhappy mood, complaining that her friends (by which it seems possible she meant her family) had 'behaved very ill to her, in consequence of her going to Bristol with a man'. By the time they got to Avon Street she seems to have been in some distress. She took most of her clothes off, but then sat on the bed 'crying very much' although she would not say why. David Price said if she did not stop immediately he would go, at which point Fanny said she would make away with herself if he did. He did not believe her. She had, he said, often spoken of killing herself. She seemed, he added, 'uncomfortable' at having left her friends, saying if it had not been for them she would not have been on the town. Despite her pleas and threats, he left. She soon followed him downstairs, throwing on her clothes in such a hurry that she was now just in her bonnet and shift, with shoes on her bare feet. Her petticoat, stays (corsets), stockings and garters were all left behind in the room in her haste to follow him. She told Hester she would be back in a quarter of an hour, and went out into the cold February night after David Price.

She caught up with him at the bottom of Avon Street, near the river, and there he bade her goodnight – and left her. We last hear Fanny's voice through the evidence of Ann Pearce, wife of the quay watchman. Between ten and eleven o'clock at night, she reported, she

Broad Quay, one of the quays between the end of Southgate Street and Avon Street, here seen in the late 1920s during a flood. Bath Record Office

heard a man calling out: 'Fanny, Fanny, Fanny!' to which a girl's voice replied, 'Well?'

'Where are you going?'

'Along here.'

'Goodnight.'

'Goodnight.'

Shortly afterwards, she heard the sound of someone falling in the water and the girl's voice crying out 'Lord save me!' Fanny's lifeless body was taken from the river soon afterwards. There was, testified Ann Pearce, a wall by the quay to prevent passers-by falling in.

Despite the fact that Fanny would have had to have climbed over the wall, despite her previous threats to kill herself, and despite her wretchedness that dreadful Saturday evening, the jury, incredibly, decided it was an accident. It is possible that there was a lot of guilt washing around at the inquest. Fanny's mother, Sophia, had had to testify about her daughter's previous life, and she must have been feeling overwhelmed with distress, not just at having thrown her out of her home, but at hearing about the terrible existence to which her daughter had been reduced. But it is possible there were some uncomfortable feelings amongst the jury. How many of those upright citizens had visited one of the Avon Street brothels? If they had, Fanny's story must have been an unpleasant reminder of the grief and pain their actions caused. Surely Avon Street prostitutes did not commit suicide? Much better to decide it was an accident. After all, she had cried out 'Lord save me!' The jury did not seem to consider that it might have been her soul rather than her body she wanted the Lord to save. Accident or suicide, the tragic figure of Fanny Dayer tells us what it was really like to be a 'nymph of Avon Street'. She was just eighteen years old.

The inexplicable death of Thomas Haverfield

Our next story dates from 1831, and concerns Thomas Haverfield, an apparently prosperous gentleman who lived in Devonshire Buildings, a late Georgian terrace on the south side of Bath. Although not in the most fashionable part of the city, these are still large, desirable houses. Haverfield, a well-built man of about 5 feet 8 inches, with an aquiline nose and thick hair going grey, seems to have been liked by his servants, and he, apparently, trusted them. However, as one of the servants, Mary Gay, told the inquest, he had recently been subject to fits, and his behaviour had changed. He was often intoxicated, and for this to have been worthy of note at that period, he must have been very intoxicated indeed. He had been drinking considerable amounts of brandy, sometimes neat, sometimes mixed with water or with beer. His neighbour, Joseph Large, had also become concerned about his state of health. He had known Thomas Haverfield for fourteen years, but in the last two or three months he was much altered, and seemed at times, 'not in his senses'.

At 10.00 pm, on the evening of Thursday 24th March 1831, having finished his dinner, Haverfield once again drank a quantity of brandy. He then called in his servant Mary Gay to count his money, which amounted to three £5 notes and a gold sovereign. While £16 might not buy you much of a night out today, he actually had in his hand the equivalent of over £1,000, in modern terms. Mr Haverfield does not seem to have had any lack of ready money. The question that leaps to mind is – why did he get Mary to check his money? Was he already so drunk that he could not count it himself? If so, it did not stop him going out. Mary put the money in a crimson silk purse, and handed it to her employer. Dressed smartly in black trousers and a brown coat and sporting a black neckerchief, he placed the purse into the pocket of his velvet waistcoat, put on his hat and great coat, picked up his stick, got into a fly carriage and went into Bath. His servants must have watched his departure anxiously. He had been out all the previous night, only returning home during the day, and they were clearly becoming very worried about him.

The next time we see Thomas Haverfield is in Milsom Street, then, as now, Bath's principal shopping street. He went to billiard rooms run by Mr Bedford at No. 17. Haverfield was here from 11.00 pm to 2.00 am, betting at billiards. He lost, and to drown his sorrows had a noggin, or quarter pint, of brandy mixed with beer. By now he was extremely drunk. John Bedford, the son of the owner, was reluctant to serve him but Haverfield insisted. However, he must have persuaded him to leave, and John Barber, a billiard-marker, saw him off the premises. He too seems to have been concerned about him, for Haverfield was now staggering as he walked. Barber remembered that two years previously Haverfield had had a fit while playing billiards, and it seemed to him that he had never properly recovered. He subsequently, Barber added, frequently appeared out of his mind and delirious. John Barber watched him at the top of Milsom Street, talking to a gentleman, who then went on to the York House, now a Travelodge, while Thomas Haverfield went down Milsom Street. It is our last view of Thomas Haverfield alive.

Early next morning some quarrymen on their way to work discovered a coat, black hat and stick by the Old Bridge, which Haverfield would have crossed on his way home. They took the items to work and showed their boss what they had found. Meanwhile, at Devonshire Buildings, the worried household waited in vain for their master to return. When a couple of days passed without any sight of him, they advertised in the *Bath Journal* of 4 April, giving his description and seeking an account of his whereabouts. The news came almost immediately. Haverfield's corpse had been pulled from the river and taken to a riverside pub, the *Duke of York*, where two days later, on 6 April, the inquest was held. The purse was still in his waistcoat pocket, now only containing one £5 note, the sovereign and some small change. There was no farewell note, but the fact that he had removed his coat and hat, carefully placing them next to his stick on the ground, indicated a deliberate intention to end it all. Had he just fallen in, he would still have been wearing the coat, and the hat and stick would have been in the river with him. Clearly, he had not been attacked and robbed. Equally clearly, his behaviour, both in the weeks leading up to his death and on that night, shows that something was badly wrong. The inquest jury came to the conclusion that he had taken his own life because he was 'not of sound mind, memory or understanding, but lunatic and distracted'. But there is something strangely baffling about this story. You can almost hear the mystification in the witnesses' voices. Haverfield was wealthy. Why did he not seek medical advice? Limited as it then was, it still might have

Devonshire Buildings, seen here as they would have looked in Haverfield's time – a rather elegant terrace in the middle of countryside. Bath Central Library

been some help. If he had troubles, why did he not confide in someone? He was certainly very drunk indeed, but he had been drunk before, and not taken his own life. Why on that night, of all nights, did the burden of life become just too much for Thomas Haverfield?

John Hanning Speke – accident or suicide?

In September 1864 a coroner's inquest was held at Monks Park, a family seat near Corsham, in Wiltshire. If the coroner, Mr Kemm, thought that, with the verdict of accidental death, the sad affair would be put to rest, he was totally wrong. From the start, rumours of suicide abounded, as they still do today. Other gossip about the deceased and the man with whom his name will always be linked, the explorer Richard Burton, added fuel to the fire, and as recently as 1990, a film called *Mountains of the Moon* combined all the more sensational elements attributed to him. The story, which was to end in a windswept field in Wiltshire, began in Aden in 1854, where the charismatic explorer Richard Burton was preparing an expedition to Africa, one of his aims being to discover more about the source of the Nile. Suddenly he heard of the death of his trusted friend Stocks,

John Hanning Speke. Author's collection

who was to accompany him. Burton urgently needed someone to fill his place, and he was introduced to an ambitious young Indian Army officer, who, it was suggested, would be a useful travelling companion. His name was John Hanning Speke.

On the surface, Speke seemed like a good choice. He was a brave, experienced soldier, and a very good shot, indeed he was almost a professional hunter. He had even done some surveying in Tibet and China. What's more, he was keen to go. Burton had his doubts. Speke's surveying methods had the reputation of being somewhat slapdash, he had little interest in the African people, regarding them as primitive aborigines (this is clear from a book by Speke, published in 1863), and, somewhat alarmingly, he declared he was so bored with life that he had come to Africa to be killed. Yet Burton was in urgent need of an extra man. He accepted the young man's offer. The first expedition was to Somaliland, and on their return, the cracks in the relationship began to show.

Burton's plans were interrupted by the Crimean War, in which both men served. After the war Burton returned to Africa. Somewhat surprisingly, he decided that he would again offer Speke the chance to come with him. Speke accepted – a fateful decision for both of them.

The expedition nearly came to grief on a number of occasions. Every danger that can be imagined on such an enterprise occurred. Speke began to be frustrated by Burton. Hearing of a large lake from which a river flowed northwards, Speke was eager to visit it – Burton, given the by now parlous state of the expedition, was more cautious. But, finally, to relieve Speke's boredom, he allowed him to investigate. When Speke returned, he was certain that this was the African explorer's Holy Grail – the lake, which would later be named Lake Victoria, was, he declared, the source of the Nile. Burton, contrary to what many think, did not deny this – he simply doubted that Speke had sufficient evidence. He had not even seen whether water left or entered the lake – it was all hearsay. Burton tried to persuade Speke that they would return, but first they should regain their health and gather new resources. The expedition had to leave with the matter unresolved. By the time the two got back to Aden, their apparent friendship was all on the surface. Beneath lay an irreconcilable division. The presence of a naval vessel returning to England gave Speke the chance to return home without Burton, who was making the journey about a fortnight later.

Speke did not waste his head start. He hastened to the Royal Geographical Society, explained his discovery and secured the right to lead the next expedition to Lake Victoria. In 1860, Speke set out once again for Lake Victoria, this time with the easy-going Captain James Grant. Perhaps afraid that Grant might steal his glory, Speke sent him off on another investigation, which established the source of the White Nile, while he alone revisited Lake Victoria. Once again, his investigations were far from perfect. Yet as far as he was concerned, he had triumphed. 'The Nile is settled,' he cabled the Royal Geographical Society on his way home in 1862. At first he was a hero. But then the doubts and criticisms began to emerge, most significantly from an angry Richard Burton.

The stage was set for a showdown, and that showdown was due to take place in Bath. To the city's great excitement, the British Association for the Advancement of Science held its annual meeting there in 1864. The weekly paper produced a daily edition during the event, with full details of all the debates and lectures. The place was packed with eminent scientists, but many regarded the highlight as an event scheduled for 16 September. The differences between Burton and Speke were to be settled with a debate between the two about the source of the Nile. To add piquancy, the moderator was to be David Livingstone – who himself was now becoming interested in the Nile's true source. On being told of the plan, Speke reportedly said: 'If Burton appears on the platform at Bath, I shall kick him!'

The day before the debate was due, Burton and his wife entered the hall – and found themselves face to face with Speke. No words passed between them, but after a short time Speke was seen to become restless in his seat, finally jumping up and leaving, with a cry of 'Oh, I cannot stand this any longer!' When asked if he would be retuning to his place he replied 'I hope not!' With that he left the room, bidding Sir Roderick Murchison, the President of the Geographical Society, farewell, and promising to be back for the next day's debate.

Early that evening, a rumour began to circulate that Speke had been involved in a shooting accident, but many ignored it. Next day, at the appointed hour of 11.00 am, the room was crowded with an expectant audience – but there was no sign of Speke. After about ten minutes, a shaken and emotional Murchison came to the platform to announce

It was from Neston Park that Hanning Speke set out to go shooting. The author

that there would be no debate. The rumour was true. John Hanning Speke was dead.

The story that finally emerged was this. Speke had been staying with his brother at Monks Park, near Corsham, about ten miles from Bath. After leaving the conference in an apparently distressed state of mind, he had gone shooting partridges at a place called Wadswick, not far from Neston Park, the home of his cousin George Fuller. They had set out about 2.30 pm, with Speke carrying his own gun, a Lancaster breech-loader, which had no safety guard. However, one of the witnesses, the gamekeeper Daniel Davis, asserted that he thought it was safe. At about 4.00 pm, George Fuller climbed over a low wall, about two feet high, and walked on. After he had gone about sixty yards, he heard a gun shot and turned.

'I saw the deceased standing on the same part of the wall which I had previously got over. He was without his gun and shortly afterwards fell into the field which I was in.' Fuller ran up to him and according to him found the deceased sensible. Speke murmured: 'Don't move me.' They were his last words. Fuller stayed with him for about five minutes and then went to seek help, leaving him in the care of the keeper. Fuller noted: 'I observed his gun lying in the field that I

It is unclear whether Speke was negotiating the stile, or the wall where the monument to him now stands. The latter seems the most likely. The author

and the deceased were in. One barrel – the right – was then at half cock – the left had been discharged. I heard very little report and I should suppose the muzzle of the gun was very near the body of the deceased when it went off.'

Mr Snow, a surgeon from the nearby village of Box described the wound: 'It was on the left side, such as would be made by a cartridge if the muzzle of the gun was close to the body. There was no other wound. It led in a direction upwards and towards the spine, passing through the lungs.' It had not touched the heart, but Speke must literally have drowned in his own blood.

The inquest was held at his brother's house. Not only was Speke himself a national hero, but his brother was a well-known landowner. It was never going to be easy for Mr Kemm the coroner and the inquest jury to find a verdict other than accidental death, and that is indeed what happened. But were they right? Almost immediately the stories began to fly around. Firstly, Burton was accused of lack of feeling, despite having made a conciliatory statement the next day expressing his 'sincere feelings of admiration of his [Speke's] character and enterprise' and his 'deep sense of his loss now that he is so suddenly and shockingly removed from his geographical associates.' This was clearly not enough for some newspaper reporters. Although he kept a fairly calm exterior, his wife later wrote that he wept long and bitterly over what had happened and that she had had to comfort him for days afterwards.

But the story which has lasted most persistently is that this was no accident. Burton himself wrote darkly to a friend that Speke had 'come to a bad end and no one knows anything about it'. It is easy to see why suicide was being suggested. Speke was an excellent and experienced shot. He had pursued game in various parts of the world without coming to grief. Why should he suddenly be so careless with his shotgun while crossing a low wall? He was very distressed and anxious about the coming debate. He must have known that there were others, besides Burton, who were critical of his expedition. Public speaking did not come easily to him – Burton was a fluent and powerful debater. He had also once been Speke's mentor, and had certainly saved his life through careful nursing when he had almost died of fever in Africa. As one modern writer, Quentin Keynes has eloquently put it: 'the double-headed spectre of guilt and dread' must have been stalking him that September afternoon. And so, say the suicide theorists, Speke shot himself deliberately.

However, several facts need to be borne in mind. Firstly, gun safety was much more lax then than it is today. People were accustomed to going around carrying loaded guns. Muzzle-loaders, for example, could not be unloaded – people would fire off any unused shot at the end of the day. People were advised not to go shooting with a sore foot – some had been tempted to use their guns as walking sticks, with predictable results. Secondly, if you are going to use a shotgun to kill yourself, it is usual to aim at the head. Shooting yourself in the chest is a very unpredictable method. It can result in horrible injuries, but not necessarily death. Thirdly, crossing a wall with a shotgun was dangerous. Six months previously, a man at Great Waldingfield in Suffolk had shot and killed himself while crossing a stile in an almost identical accident, and no one ever suggested it was suicide. But he was just a farm bailiff and not a national hero.

This is a possible reconstruction of what happened that day – its details fit all the known facts. Speke came to the wall and began to climb over. As he reached the top, he lowered the butt of the gun towards the ground on the far side to support himself. He may well have slipped on the loose stones of the drystone wall and instinctively used the gun to save himself. As he went to retrieve the gun by pulling it up by its muzzle, the trigger caught on a projecting stone or tough plant, thus causing the barrel to discharge. This would explain why the body and the gun were in the same field, why the muzzle was so

The monument states firmly that it was an accident. That is almost certainly true.
The author

close to the body when the gun discharged, and the angle of the wound. But it does not explain why such an experienced hunter was so careless. The answer lies surely in Speke's agitated, distracted state. When carrying a loaded shotgun, especially one without a safety guard, it is essential to have your wits about you and your mind on the job in hand. Speke's mind that fateful September afternoon was not focussed on hunting or gun safety – it was in a turmoil about the ordeal facing him the next day. He simply lost concentration.

'Men say I killed him,' Burton is supposed to have said – and in a way he had. Perhaps the most accurate verdict would have been that it was an accidental death while the balance of the mind was disturbed.

Hanning had travelled the world and seen strange sights, but this very English view of a high, bleak, Wiltshire plateau, was the last he was to see. Or was his mind too in too much turmoil to notice? The author

That might have allowed Speke's memory to rest in peace, but it was not open to the jury to say that. The simple verdict of accidental death allowed the conspiracy theorists to get busy. They are still at it today, and it is unlikely that this sober assessment will make the least bit of difference. A mystery is so much more interesting.

CHAPTER 10

The Wellsway Pit Disaster

An unexplained crime

When one thinks of Somerset today, coal mining is not an industry that leaps to mind. Yet the Somerset coalfield was active right up until the 1970s, and there were coal mines on the outskirts of Bath until about 1880. Life was even tougher for Somerset coal miners than it was for many Welsh miners, as the seams of coal were narrow and deep underground. Boys were employed to pull the coal from the coal face to the waiting trucks using the dreaded guss and crook. The guss was a harness that went around the waist, while the crook was the hook on the end of a strap which hooked on to the trolleys which the unfortunate boys had to pull along. This meant crawling on their hands and knees with the strap or rope going between their legs, the trolley following on behind. The heat caused by being so far below the surface added to the misery. It was said you could tell a Somerset coal miner by the band of toughened skin around his waist, caused by the rubbing of the guss. This device was still being used within living memory. There was, too, the risk of disaster, caused by gas, roof falls or flooding. Yet this tough life engendered a camaraderie among the men. Even when two villages were traditional rivals, such as Radstock and Midsomer Norton, where the blood fields were so called because of the bare-knuckle fighting that went on there between men and boys from the two places, below ground no one would ever have endangered another man's life. That is why the terrible events of November 1839 are so etched on the memory of this now green and pleasant valley. On Friday 8 November 1839, twelve people, ranging in ages from twelve to forty-four, were deliberately murdered at their work place, the Wellsway Pit between Radstock and Midsomer Norton. To this day no one has ever been able to explain why it happened, or discovered who was responsible.

The early morning shift in 1839 started at 4.00 am, when twelve men went down to relieve the night team which consisted of seven men. Lowering men into the pit was carried out by the hooker system: each man sat in a loop of rope, sometimes with a boy on his lap, and the loop was attached to the winding rope. In 1839 this was a single

Radstock colliers at Norton Hill colliery. Note the wide range of ages. Author's collection

Radstock, a mining town among the green hills of Somerset. Trains carrying coal can be seen in the middle foreground with slag. Author's collection

Some measure of how tough and how united the Radstock miners were perceived to be is given by the number of police called in to deal with any demonstrations during the 1912 strike. Author's collection

flat, ribbon-like rope made of four cables of twisted hemp. It was five inches wide and one and a quarter inches thick. Waiting to hook themselves on to the rope that morning were Richard Langford, aged forty-four, and his two sons Farnham, sixteen and Alfred, thirteen. Another father working with two sons was James Keevil, forty-one, with his sons Mark, fifteen and James, fourteen. Alongside them were William Adams, nineteen, William Sumers, twenty-six, John Barnett, forty-one, James Pearce, eighteen, and two more youngsters, Amos Dando, thirteen, and the baby of the team, Leonard Dowling, just twelve years old.

On the previous night, the shifts had changed over without any problems. George Kingston, the bailiff at the pit, had watched the men go down. He left the pit at 8.15 pm but slept at the works and heard no noise during the night. Another miner, John Fricker, had also been at the pit until 8.00 pm, and saw nothing untoward. The next morning, the men went through their normal procedures, but as Thomas James pulled back the covering over the pit mouth, he heard the ropeman, William Saunders, say, 'What is the matter with the rope?' He looked up and could not see anything wrong, so replied that nothing was the matter. He could not have been more wrong. As the rope took the weight of the twelve men, it snapped, the end coming out of the pit with great force on to the tiles of the shed where Kingston was standing. The twelve men fell 252 yards to the bottom, smashing against the sides of the shaft as they fell. Their bodies were so dashed to pieces that the horrified rescuers could only identify one body with any certainty. All the rest were smashed and dismembered. The night shift, who had been waiting at the bottom were so shocked by the sight that they were found 'speechless and stupefied' by the rescuers.

As news spread, people started to gather at the pit. Among them was Thomas Hill, who had come to offer his services as rescuer. He was puzzled by the accident, for he too had been at the pit the previous evening and seen the rope in working order. The only conclusion was that the rope had been tampered with.

News of the disaster soon reached the families of the twelve men, who turned up, hoping for good news. There was none. The *Bath Chronicle* reported that:

It is quite impossible to describe the scene which ensued. The shrieks and wailings of the poor creatures were truly heart-rending, particularly when it was discovered it was impossible to tell one body from another.

Of the families, Langford left a widow and two children, Keevil a widow and five children, and Barnett a widow and seven children.

Inspection of the rope revealed that it had been chipped nearly in two during the night. Almost certainly it had been deliberately cut, and in such a way as to hide the fact that anything was wrong. The newspaper report explained for those unfamiliar with a winding rope and could not understand why the fault was not noticed:

Those who are at all acquainted with the strength, thickness and general construction of these ropes are aware it would be easy to weaken and damage them with a blunt instrument so that they would preserve the outward appearance of their usual strength, but would snap when the ordinary weight was placed upon them.

Where the rope gave way, the fibres were jagged and uneven in the part they had not been tampered with, but in the rest were as even and level as if a knife or chisel had passed over and into them.

The *Chronicle* reporter spoke to several miners who thought that it had been laid on a stone and hit by a crowbar.

Despite torrents of rain, crowds turned up at the funeral, which took place at St John's Church, Midsomer Norton. The bodies were placed in unmarked coffins, for no one could be sure which body was which. They lie together in one grave – there really was no other option for the grieving families. The colliery paid for the coffins and a collection was held for the families, but this was a poor neighbour-

In pouring rain, the funeral procession climbed this hill to the church of St John, Midsomer Norton. The author

hood, and although people gave what they could, it did not amount to much. And during the funeral the two the questions at the back of everyone's minds must have been – Who? Why?

Despite the coalmasters of Radstock putting up a reward of £100, the culprit was never found, nor has an explanation ever come to light. George Kingston, the bailiff, was asked if there were tensions between the men. The coroner was probably thinking about the rivalry between Radstock and Midsomer Norton, for miners from both towns worked at the pit. Kingston assured him that not only did he know of no ill-feeling between the men, he had always considered them to be on a most friendly footing. One suggestion was that it was an attack on the mine manager, for there had been been friction between men and management. But would a dissident risk killing his friends and workmates for the sake of murdering a man who might or might not – and indeed was not – on that shift? It seems extremely unlikely. It remains totally baffling.

At least some good came out of the disaster. It was immediately decided that a loaded bucket would be lowered at the start of each shift to test the rope. Further safety measure soon followed, such as a safety rope supporting the main rope. Then wire ropes were introduced, and cages for men to descend and ascend, in July 1854. These cages, which had four decks, carried ten men and in the case of an

The single grave of the twelve victims. The author

The old stone was renewed by Somerset coal miners in 1953. The author

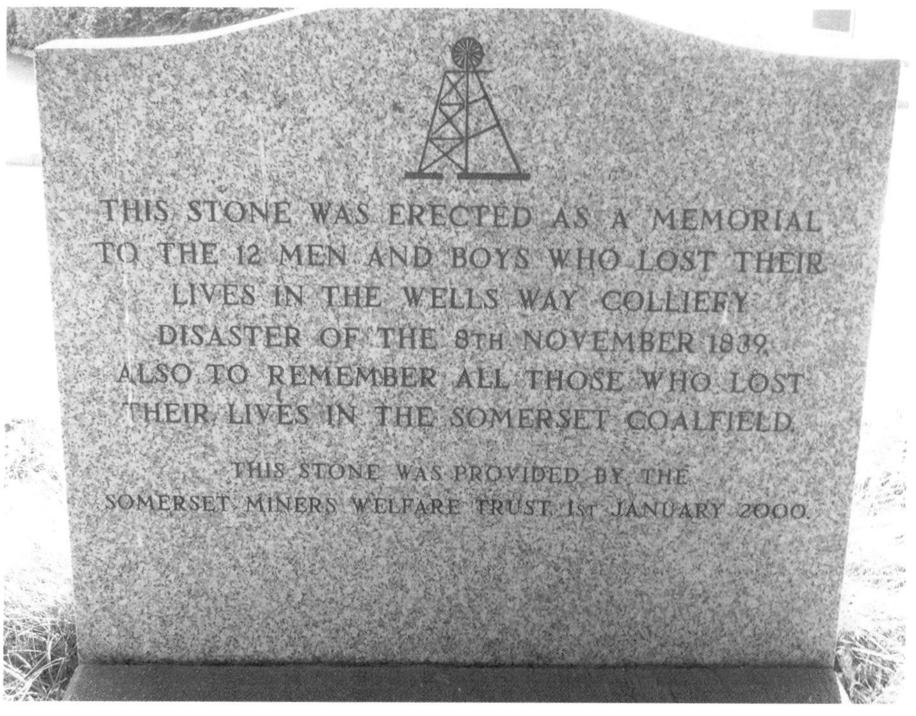

A new stone was added in 2000 to commemorate all those who lost their lives in the Somerset coalfield. The author

accident the men were offered some sort of protection. Under the hooker system, there was none.

The grave of those who died in the Wellsway Pit Disaster has a memorial with the following words:

> *In this grave is deposited the remains of the 12 under-mentioned sufferers, all of whom were killed at Wells Way coal works on the 8th November, 1839, by the snapping of the rope as they were on the point of descending into the pit. The rope was generally believed to have been maliciously cut.*

The headstone is cared for by the Somerset Miners Association and was renewed in 2000. Never were the words 'Their memory lives on' more apt.

CHAPTER 11

Two Unresolved Mysteries

The corpse in the cave & The Southstoke scandal

The final chapter of this book deals with fictional crime set in and around the city of Bath. It is rare, in crime novels for the story to be unresolved, even if, occasionally there is a giveaway to the reader that perhaps the wrong person has been caught. If that does happen, this in itself provides the story line for another book. It may be a cliché to say that life is not like that, but like most clichés, it happens to be true. This chapter deals with two unresolved (rather than unsolved) mysteries. In the second, it demonstrates how historical researchers are themselves detectives, and as with police invstigations, the trail can sometimes go cold. In the first, a murder was committed, and a man was arrested. But no one ever stood trial. It is the story of . . .

The corpse in the cave – the murder of Elsie Adeline Luke

On a sunny weekend, even in winter, Hampton Rocks is a popular spot. Follow the National Trust's Skyline walk, as many people do, and you come to a section of what at first sight seem to be rocky outcrops and caves on a hillside overlooking the Limpley Stoke valley. In fact, this is an industrial landscape. Many years ago this was quarried for Bath Stone, and the course of an old tramway which took the stone down to the canal below can still be traced, descending the steep hillside. By 1840 all work had ceased, and it became a picnic spot and a popular area for children to play. Today, our concerns about health and safety have resulted in many of the caverns being closed off for they are prone to roof collapses. We would certainly not advise parents to let children play there unattended – and rightly so. But in 1891, young Frank Clark often went up there with his friends to play among the rocks, especially during the summer holidays. He was there on 7 August, just a few days after his elder brother, Arthur, had enjoyed an August Bank Holiday picnic among the crags with some friends. On this occasion Frank discovered a lady's black fancy open work straw hat. Although a trifle damp, it was rather smart, turned up

The cave as it was when Elsie's body was found there. Bath Central Library

at back and side, and trimmed in black and cream. He decided to take it home to give to his mother, but she immediately took against it.

'I believe it belongs to someone who has been murdered – it shan't stay in the house,' she declared. This was, as it turned out, a remarkably accurate guess, but doubtless the police officer, to whom the Clark family showed the hat, thought it was a lot of fuss about nothing, although he duly made a note of it and put the hat away. No one thought any more about it. They forgot about a strange incident which had occurred at Arthur's picnic, when an agitated young man walked past, bareheaded and without a jacket or waistcoat. It tells us much about the social mores of the time that this was considered noteworthy. When asked if he was in trouble, he replied that he had been bathing in the River Avon, and someone had stolen his outer clothes and his hat. With that, he walked on. This explanation puzzled the picnic party, for the river was over a mile away, at the bottom of a steep hill.

Two years went by. The hat, stored by the police officer, was mislaid – almost certainly thrown away. Boys continued to make Hampton Rocks an adventure playground. They clambered among the fallen boulders, and the more daring explored the caves. In late September 1893, Cecil Brand and a school friend called Emerson scrambled into just such a cavern. If they had been hoping to find buried treasure they were disappointed. What they did find, however, as they pushed aside the flat stones which covered the floor of the

The same cave today. The author

cave, was something far more dramatic. It was the body of a young woman.

Once the boys had run and told their parents, the police were soon on the scene. Easing himself into the larger of the two entrances of the cave, Police Sergeant Charles Edwards found a body hidden under flat stones. It was mainly a skeleton, lying face down, with the left knee drawn up. The hair, light brown in colour, was attached to the skull, still in a plait fixed with rusted pins. When examined, it fell into short pieces, where it had been chewed by rodents. Of the clothing, the white corsets were in a fair state and there were shreds of other clothes, some marked H Kerry. The shoes, which were Oxford brogues of good quality, were still on the feet. Any doubt that this was anything other than murder was removed by the fact that the skull had been broken by a blow over left eye leaving a fracture the size of a penny.

A clue to how long the body had been lying there was a collection of little springs, which were identified as a bustle. This particular style of underwear was going out of fashion by 1890, and not worn after 1891. The pathetic fragments of what had once been a living woman were removed to the *George* at Bathampton, where the inquest was held.

The police surgeon announced that he believed that this was the body of a young woman aged between nineteen and twenty-one who was just over five foot in height. Cecil Brand was called to describe his discovery of the body, but the witness with the most sensational tale to tell was a man known to his friends as 'Colonel' Dill. He was a time-keeper and clerk but he also had a part-time job at the rifle butts on Bathampton Down, above the quarries, marking the targets and clearing up spent cartridges. He would also wander around the down, looking for items of value which he would sell. He was, in fact, a

The pathetic remains of Elsie were carried into this inn yard – the George *at Bathampton.* The author

totter. He probably found it necessary to augment his earnings for he was, as became obvious during later proceedings, a man who was fond of the bottle. On top of all that, hints were dropped that there was another reason for his wanderings around Bathampton Down. He was described as being 'not a man for the ladies', his friends were exclusively male, and he had a little hut near the shooting range where he could sleep – or meet fellow wanderers. In an age when respectability was important, all these little things began to tell against him –

not least because he came from a well respected Bath family of butchers and shopkeepers. When the jury heard his evidence, things began to look very black indeed for 'Colonel' Dill.

Thanks to information tendered by Dill, the police had recovered a lady's cuffs and handkerchief, both bloodstained, and a gold watch which had once had a chain. Dill told the inquest jury how he had been strolling on the down about two years ago and at 8.00 am one Friday discovered these items. As later became clear, they were found not far from the cave. His plan was to sell the watch and chain, but although he did this with the chain, he raffled the watch at the *Exeter Inn*, in Southgate Street. Miss Cotterell, the landlord's daughter, won the watch and it was recovered from her. It was 14 carat gold and prettily chased. Her father, Timothy Cotterell, remembered the raffle because the glass was broken and he had told Dill he should have it repaired first, which had been done. He remembered, too that Dill said it had come from his sister.

Dill recalled that the cuff had a small solitaire, which he described as 'a trumpery thing'. Nevertheless, inspired by his finds, he and a friend called Field had searched for more, but without success. By this time the inquest jury was becoming suspicious of Dill. The foreman and another juror said they thought it was very strange that he had not reported these finds to the police. Dill, suddenly sensing danger, said hastily that he and Field had shown some police who were among the volunteers using the rifle range. Pressed, he was unable to remember which ones. He added that he could describe of lots of things he had picked up there, and that he slept up there when marking to pick up spent cases first thing. The foreman promptly asked if he slept in a cave.

'No I never slept in a cave thank you. I have a hut and a bed up there,' replied Dill. This flippant attitude did not help his case. Fortunately for Mr Dill, not only were the police able to establish that he had a credible alibi, but were also following a trail which led to the identity of the unknown girl – and the discovery of a new suspect.

The handkerchief was marked AH Kerry, and letters which formed part of this name were found on other items. Not unnaturally, it was at first thought that this was the girl's name, but A H Kerry was very much alive. She was the wife of James Kerry of Cheriton House, Oldfield Park, whose maid, Elsie Wilkie had left under strange circumstances in July 1891. She had been under notice but had declared she wanted to quit anyway because her uncle in London had died leaving her money. She had gone away for the weekend before her notice had run out, but had not returned on the Monday. The Kerry family had assumed she had just left early, although she had left a box containing letters, which they threw away. However, she had been

Elsie Luke. Bath Central Library

seen in Bath in the vicinity of Kingsmead Terrace. Further investigations showed that Elsie had earlier worked for a Mr Dykes, a superintendent on the Somerset and Dorset Railway. She had told them that Wilkie was the name of her stepfather who had brought her up, and that her real surname was Luke. When the police tried to trace the address she had given in London, however, it was false. Mr Kerry told them she was remarkably well spoken and knew some French. She was engaged as a cook and seemed well behaved until they discovered that she stole things – including clothes. On the last Saturday of July she had gone to the house of Andrew Dillon, telling him that her master was away and she would like to board at his house. The last time she was seen was when she went for a walk on August Bank Holiday, but the Dillons were able to tell the police that she frequently visited the Railway Mission Hall, that she was prone to fainting fits, and that she had once been engaged to a young man called Coombs – an engagement that had been broken off. Since it had now been shown that Dill had marched with the volunteers to a training camp at Devizes over the Bank Holiday weekend, and had been there all week, attention now began to focus on Arthur Stephenson Coombs, a young man of twenty, still working his apprenticeship at the carriage works of S & A Fuller in Kingsmead Street.

The picture that the police were building of Elsie Luke – or Wilkie, as many of the witnesses would call her – was of a young woman who was not only a thief but also a consummate liar. At Mrs Restarick's Servant Registry in Northumberland Place, for example, she had given her name as Elizabeth Luke, working at No. 38 Hungerford Road, Lower Weston where she had been employed as a plain cook. When the police tried to follow up the reference she had given, of a Mrs Davy in Brighton, no answer was received, and they were finally told that Mrs Davy had gone. Mrs Bryant, of No. 61 Hungerford Road worked with her for a time at the Irish Linen Warehouse, when Elsie had given her age as twenty-five. She recalled she was highly nervous and prone to fainting fits, which was why she had left. She too remembered that Elsie had said she was engaged to Coombs. With this and further evidence that would be revealed at the committal proceedings, the police decided they had enough to arrest Coombs, who was charged with murder.

The proceedings were held before the Bath magistrates in the courthouse at Weston, with Mr Titley defending. The first witness was Mrs Kerry who said that Elsie Luke had said she was twenty-two. She was a superior looking girl, but she sometimes felt faint and would go into the garden. Unfortunately, although in many ways she was a good and efficient cook and maid, she had stolen clothes, and on the day she had left, they had discovered that a dress Mrs Kerry had bought for her daughter's birthday had gone. Mr John Edwards, a fishmonger, said that he had seen Coombs and Elsie Luke at the Railway Mission Hall in Monmouth Street. He had seen the two together at the outing to Sidmouth but he remembered that at one time Coombs had said of her that she ought to be dead and buried, although he could not remember when the comment had been made. He had not seen them together for a time.

Arthur Stephenson Coombs. Bath Central Library

Kate Bullock, the housemaid at the Kerrys' said she knew 'Wilkie', as she called her, had a young man but she could not remember if it was Coombs. However, she did remember that in the week before she left, Wilkie had taken two bundles down the garden and handed them over the fence to a young girl. Dill was then called, but was so drunk that he was told to give evidence at another time. Then came Annie Hayman, the wife of an engine driver, who said that she knew both the deceased and the prisoner. She said that Elsie had come to her house on the Saturday before the Bank Holiday and asked to stay, but as this was impossible she had sent her to Dillon's. The girl had said that the Kerrys would pay for her lodgings as they were going away but she also told her that she was three months pregnant. Mrs Hayman assumed that it was Coombs's child, for Elsie spoke with him on the Sunday. When she had disappeared, everyone thought she had returned to Cheriton House.

The police then presented as evidence letters they had found at Coombs' house, along with a brooch that belonged to Elsie. The letters were from a young lady with which he associated, called Pollie Shephard. Pollie, it is clear, had no time at all for Elsie Luke. 'She is a beast of a girl,' she wrote in one letter. She was scornful of her claims of pregnancy and her fainting fits. Her opinion of those was that Elsie could faint when she liked. She also had heard (correctly as it turned out) that Elsie had been to prison and then sent to an industrial school. But for all Elsie's attendance at the railway mission, Pollie did not believe that she had been converted. On 19 July a cold tone crept into her letters, and she accused Coombs of being two-faced and a deceiver, but she was soon back to addressing him as Dearest Arthur.

The prosecuting solicitor then raised the question of an injury to Arthur Coombs' hand, which he had allegedly suffered on 5 August. It was severe enough for him to go the casualty ward, where it was described as a human bite. Meanwhile, the police had uncovered further evidence about Elsie herself. Pollie's suspicions were quite right. Elsie Luke had been the inmate of the Girls' Reformatory at Limpley Stoke. She had been sentenced in 1880, when she was just fourteen years old, to ten days imprisonment and five years detention. Teachers at the school said she was possessed of a violent temper.

The continuing reports in the newspapers were exciting enormous interest, and crowds went out to Hampton Rocks to view the scene of the crime. Adding to the crowds were vendors of food and drink, eager to cash in.

The inquest resumed on 12 October, and this time Dill was sober enough to strengthen his alibi by saying he had been helping the Reverend Shickle at the camp at Devizes over the Bank Holiday weekend. He was definitely not on Hampton Rocks. Coombs should have been at the camp, as he was a Volunteer, but had elected not to

PORTRAITS OF THE VICTIM AND THE ACCUSED.

SURROUNDINGS OF THE CAVE.

THE OPENING TO THE CAVE.

THE INTERIOR OF THE CAVE.

From the Bath Chronicle. Bath Central Library

go that year. Annie Hayman then took the stand, to state that Elsie Luke and Arthur Coombs were engaged. Mr Titley queried whether this was evidence or just hearsay, but the coroner said it was admissible. She went on to say that she had seen them together on 2 August, and she had certainly seen them together in May 1891 on another Mission outing to Conkwell Woods. Her daughter Lucy said the outing was in 1890, but she had seen them together in July 1891. In court, in Weston, other witnesses said they had seen them in a wood leading from Warminster Road to Hampton Down. Mr Titley, who seemed to feel that all this rather contradictory evidence was getting nowhere, said the prisoner should be discharged, having been held for a fortnight. The magistrates refused on the grounds that Mr Coombs should be allowed to clear his name – and refused bail.

The court proceedings were now running concurrently with the inquest, and at the latter, James Robinson, a miller of Herbert Road, said he had been given fruit and flowers by Elsie Luke, in July, who had told him that she and Arthur Coombs were to be married. However, on Boxing Day 1890, while at a party in Oak Street where the two were together, Arthur had admitted he was not keen on her. In February 1891, Mr Dillon had seen Elsie on the doorstep of the Coombs' house, demanding to be let in and creating a scene.

Back in court, Miss Williams, of No. 33 Green Park confirmed that the two were known at the Railway

Mission. She said the outings were in 1890, and that she had not seen Coombs and Luke together after January 1891. Alfred Phillips, who had the unusual occupation of being a gymnast and clown, told rather a different story. He and a friend, Eugene Walford, had seen Coombs and Luke together on what he thought was 26 July, walking up through the woods near the Warminster road. On 27 July, the Liberal Party held a fete at Bathampton. It was here that Coombs said he had got into a fight and his thumb was injured, but a police officer said no disturbance was reported. Coombs had responded that the fight was after the police officer was there.

The prosecuting solicitor, Mr Collins, was beginning to be concerned at the quality of the evidence presented by the police, and he suddenly made an astonishing suggestion. He wanted the case dropped at the present time because if it went to trial Coombs might get off. By not committing him for trial, he could be rearrested at a later date if new evidence came to light. The magistrates were clearly unhappy with this, and decided to call Pollie Shephard – or Mary Louisa, as she was really called, on the grounds that Mr Collins had used her letters without her permission, and she had a right to explain them.

Mr Titley knew he had a good witness in Pollie – she was his wife's personal servant. He was even prepared to call his wife to back up what the girl had to say. This proved unnecessary – Pollie was quite able to look after herself. She told how Elsie Luke had attacked her and shouted at her. Despite Arthur's dalliance with Elsie, it was she, Pollie who now hoped to be married to him – an announcement greeted with applause from the public gallery. She provided Coombs with an alibi, on which she refused to be shaken. They had gone to the theatre on August Bank Holiday, at the time when the police alleged Coombs was murdering Elsie Luke. The court retired for lunch and on their return dismissed the case. Coombs was a free man.

The investigations were not over, however. There was still the inquest, which was rapidly sliding into farce. Some of the witnesses failed to turn up, or turned up late. Mrs Dillon was accused of telling Kathy Bullock not to say too much and that she knew much more. Mrs Kerry was criticised for not reading the letters found in the box which Elsie Luke had left behind before throwing them out. Mrs Hayman admitted that despite her earlier statements, her husband had reminded her that she had not known Luke personally before 1890.

Two months after the body was discovered, the inquest was still in progress, and it had now reached its most sensational stage. Arthur Stephenson Coombs elected to take the stand to make a statement. Elsie Luke, he told the jury, was not an honest woman. She had held

The canal along which Stephenson said he was walking with Miss Thorne, when others accused him of being with Elsie Luke. Andrew Swift

many posts, which she had obtained by forging references. He admitted that he had been to Cheriton House, but only to return articles, and he had only just stood inside the door. The coroner said that witnesses had seen him with a young lady in 1891 – Coombs retorted that it was not with Elsie Luke. On the Bank Holiday he had been to see off the Volunteers, and he had then gone walking with another young lady, Miss Thorne, his sister-in-law's cousin. It was with her that he had walked along the canal to Warminster Road, over Claverton Down, and back to St James's Square on 26 July. (It is astonishing how far people were prepared to walk for a gentle stroll in the days before cars were common. This is a hilly walk of at least five miles.) He insisted that he had received the injury to his thumb at the Liberal fete on 27 July. During the fireworks display two young drunks had made remarks about a lady and he had got involved in the fight. One of the men had tried to bite his leg and when he had warded him off he had bitten his hand instead. He had thought nothing of it at the time, but the bite had got worse, and eventually, on 5 August, he had gone to hospital.

He then gave an account of his bank holiday. At 8.30 am he was due to meet Miss Thorne outside the Midland Station and drive to

Thornbury, but the weather was poor, and the two had agreed not to meet if it was wet. He was indoors until 12.00 when he had been with Miss Thorne, and then after tea had had been with Miss Shephard. They had gone for a walk first and then visited the theatre. He had returned home about 10.30 pm. About a week later, Mrs Hayman had asked if he knew where Elsie Luke was and if she had gone away. He had subsequently discovered that she had stolen a dress and money. She had also sent his letters to her to Pollie's parents, who seemed remarkably relaxed about it, assuming it was a youthful indiscretion and not an engagement. Asked about Miss Thorne, he said she was just a friend, and he was showing her the town.

He was then questioned about his relationship with Elsie Luke. He sad he had met her at the Railway Mission, where she had rather pressed herself upon him. She said she received money from her family via the friend in Turleigh, but she would not let him go to Turleigh with her. At the mission, he heard how she had been to prison and reformatory, and he had begun to distance himself from her. The reason that her brooch had been found in his room because he had broken it and had meant to get it repaired for her, but she said it did not matter.

In December, the inquest finally dragged to its close. Other people who knew Elsie Luke recalled she had said she was going to marry Coombs but had said it so many times they no longer believed it. Another said that Elsie had not mentioned being pregnant to her, and she certainly did not look it.

The coroner, in summing up, had angry words for everybody. He felt that Coombs had a motive for murder, but that was not evidence. He said that Mrs Hayman's evidence could not be trusted but that Alfred Phillips was reliable. Dill, who was again inebriated, he censured for being drunk and for not having reported his finds at the time. Of Mrs Kerry he said that he believed her evidence but that it seemed marvellous to him that she had seen letters from Elise Luke and not read them. Surely a woman's curiosity should have got the better of her? Kate Bullock was fined 3 shillings for late attendance and Mrs Dillon was fined for lateness and tampering with witnesses, although he did not think she did know anything – she was just trying to make herself important. Regretfully he had to bring in an open verdict.

And that was more or less the end. On 11 December the remains of Elsie Luke were given a decent burial next to the Vicomte du Barry, who had also met a violent death. Two years later, Pollie and Arthur were married. In 1914 they went to Canada. Pollie died in Victoria in 1946, and Arthur died six years later, aged seventy-eight. Victoria is on the west coast of Canada – a very long way from Bath in an age when travel was not as easy as it is now. Why did they take that step?

Elsie lies buried not far from another victim of a violent death, the Vicomte du Barry. This is a modern replacement stone. The author

Was it just a chance for a new life and new opportunities, or had the gossip continued until it had become unbearable? No one else was ever accused of the crime. Had, perhaps, new evidence come to light which put Arthur at risk? If he had murdered Elsie Luke, only he and Pollie knew the truth – and staunch little Pollie was not going to tell.

The Southstoke scandal – the case of the notorious garden thief

In the second story, a man died of his injuries from a gunshot wound and we know who shot him. But there was an outcry when he was charged with his murder, and it has proved impossible to discover if he did stand trial.

On 4 September, James Matthews, servant of Mr Williams was employed to guard his garden at Southstoke, a village just to the south of Bath, from which fruit was being stolen. About 2.30 am he heard his dog growl, and he spotted a man in the garden taking fruit. Matthews called out a warning and caught him, but the man broke free. Matthews cried out to him to stop or he would shoot. 'Shoot and be damned!' retorted the thief. Matthews did fire, and the man exclaimed that he had been hit, but when Matthews went over to him, the thief threatened him with a stick. Reluctant to shoot again, Matthews hit him with the butt of the gun, which broke. He then went and raised the alarm.

Help arrived, including George Cleverley, the village constable at Southstoke, John Drewett, a maltster, and Anthony Aslat, a local farmer. Cleverley went to put handcuffs on the thief, whose name was Abraham Vincent, but he could not make him stand, so he removed the handcuffs, put him on a hurdle, took him to his stable and locked him in. Vincent kept saying 'Lord have mercy on me – get me a stone – let me go.' The general view of the on-lookers was that he was making a lot of fuss about nothing. Drewett said Vincent had run from Matthews, saying: 'Thee hast shot me, besn't.' He was convinced the man was shamming his wounds because he was still trying to get away. Aslat also thought he was shamming even though he had put his hand at the back of the man's trousers and found them bloody. When asked why he had not commented on this he said: 'I thought he was not as bad as he pretended to be.'

During the night, Cleverely had a look at his prisoner whom he thought obstinate and sulky. When he had a look at him the man was snoring, so Cleverely assumed he was asleep, and he himself went to bed. After about an hour, he went and had another look, and found Vincent just as he had left him, but this time he noticed blood on the man's eyebrow.

'I began to suspect he was ill,' said the constable, who seems not to have been very quick on the uptake. Still he gave him no medical care, but made him a cup of tea. Finally, when even this did not revive the prisoner, he put him in a cart and took him to the casualty hospital. The help came too late. Vincent died. The doctor said he found head injuries and shot injuries as well as a fractured bone. He came to the conclusion that it was the final blow which had killed him. The authorities decided to take prompt action. The next day, as Matthews walked down the hill into Bath, William Hall, the magistrate's officer met him by Cottage Crescent and arrested him on a charge of murder.

At the inquest a frightened Matthews refused to answer any questions put to him, which did not help his case. The jury were sympathetic, and wanted to find for manslaughter but were told they could not say that. Instead they found that Matthews was 'moved by the instigation of the devil to commit murder'.

Almost immediately there was an outcry. Vincent was notorious for stealing from gardens. As one correspondent to the local paper noted, Vincent was 'in some degree instrumental in his own death'. Matthews had done everything he could to stop Vincent without shooting, and indeed had not caused a fatal wound. It was only when Vincent threatened him with a stick that he retaliated. Then there was the lack of attention accorded to Vincent. Had he been taken straight to hospital, he might have survived. After a few editions of the paper which contain outraged letters supporting Matthews, and criticising the coroner's decision to refuse the verdict of manslaughter, the story, like Vincent, died. There is no account of what happened to Matthews. His name does not appear in accounts of the next assizes, and magistrates' records for these dates do not exist. Was the case quietly dropped? It is possible, for in December of that year, a man tried for shooting and killing a burglar was held to have acted in self-defence. Perhaps that was sufficient to save James Matthews. Perhaps the answer is out there in documents hitherto unseen or perhaps in someone's family memory. Until then, this is a story without an ending.

Chapter 12

Bath Detectives

Crimes in fiction – the writers and their detectives

Bath today is certainly not a crime-free city, although statistics show that, except for car crime, it is below the national average in the nefarious behaviour stakes. Murder is a very rare occurrence indeed. But, if you were to believe the novelists, Bath is a highly risky place to be. It has proved attractive to several well-known crime writers. Even Inspector Morse once left the bloodstained streets of Oxford to come to the elegance of the Royal Crescent, while Simon Brett's slightly sozzled actor, Charles Paris, made an appearance at the Theatre Royal. At times, fictional detectives, had they been real people, would have been tripping over one another. An American writer, Michael Z Lewin, has set several books in the city, featuring an Italian family who run a detective agency in Walcot Street while Jenni Mills has set a psychological thriller, *Crowstone*, on Combe Down. But in all these books, Bath is incidental to the story. The events could have been set elsewhere.

Four writers, however, have made the Georgian City the setting for some modern crimes, and in their books, the character of Bath is an important, indeed essential, ingredient in the narrative. Best known is Peter Lovesey's Peter Diamond, his irascible, old-style copper, who succeeds despite offending his superiors (and, indeed, his staff). In the first book, he is really rather unpleasant. Only at the end do we discover that he has an unsuspected soft centre. As the books progress, his character changes somewhat, and the reader cannot help but wonder if Peter Lovesey started to have more affection for him than he intended. He is supported by his long-suffering wife Stephanie, so his relationship with his colleague Julie Hargreaves is avuncular rather than amorous. Peter Lovesey used to live at Bradford on Avon, not far from Bath, and his love of history permeates the books as little nuggets of local interest slide their way between the pages. There is hardly a corner of the city that is not mentioned, from the Bath Clinic to Royal Victoria Park, from the canal to the Empire Hotel. Famous residents from the past do not escape being involved. Jane Austen and Mary Shelley both figure in the novels.

Christopher Lee's books also take the reader to every part of the city. However, his detective could not be different from Diamond. James Boswell Hodge Leonard is a loner, an orphan brought up in a children's home who joined the police after becoming disenchanted with a law career. He wears a tweed suite even in the hottest weather, set off by bright green socks, sports spectacles which he cleans when stressed, rides a bicycle, eats gingerbread men, and is not averse to the odd spliff. Like Diamond, however, he is disliked and even feared by superiors. Also like Diamond, he breaks the rules and kicks against pointless bureaucracy. In these books there is a romantic interest in the person of Maddy Jack, graduate of Teesside Polytechnic. Not only do famous Bath landmarks feature in his books, but also real people. David Price of Woods Restaurant appears under the name of Selsey, in a genial and well-penned portrait of an exuberant character who is thrilled to be included in the novels. Throughout Lee's books, however, runs an undercurrent of anger. Leonard is very much on the side of the underdog, and the reader soon starts to feel that writing comes from Christopher Lee's heart.

There is a problem in setting stories in an accurately portrayed city. Change takes place constantly – buildings are pulled down and shops go to new owners and assume new names. The books begin to date. The two women writers who have chosen Bath as the setting for crime write about a place that is very like the real city – but not quite. Just as you think you have pinned down a setting, you realize the description won't quite fit. This approach means that the books do not date – the city about which they are writing is as fictional as the characters, and change only occurs when the author chooses. The other difference between the men and the women is that their detectives are also women, and not police officers. However, there is no place in modern crime fiction for a Miss Marple who can outsolve the police alone and unaided. In Lizbie Brown's books, all named after styles of quilts, the American Elizabeth Blair may run a quilting shop called Martha Washington but she also has shares in the detective agency on the floor above. Max Shephard, who runs the agency knows Andy Cooper, a useful police contact, even if, as Elizabeth remarks, he is nice boy 'but if he were a horse Andy would be wearing blinkers'. The central character of the books by Morag Joss is more in line with the image of the well-meaning amateur. Sara Selkirk is a cellist, but as the books develop you realize she is not really a detective at all. Her ideas are often completely wrong, but her thoughts and reflections inspire and provoke her lover, DCI Poole, leading him to solve the crimes.

Both writers' books are full of surprises. Morag Joss is much more interested in relationships, and how interactions between people cause unexpected tensions. There are lyrical passages as well as some grim descriptions of scenes of crimes. In one truly shocking account of the aftermath of a letter bomb, the rather poetic words add to the horror rather than diminishing it. By contrast, Lizbie Brown's books can seem almost cosy – she herself pokes fun at Elizabeth by having Max describe her shop as rather twee – which makes the occasional unexpected violence all the more shocking. Of all the writers, her characters are perhaps the most normal, and they develop interestingly from book to book. Of the others, we have already seen that Diamond began to get away from his writer and take on a different character, and one senses this even more with the other two writers. Both have ended the series after only three books, and in each case one feels that the personalities of Leonard and Selkirk changed in ways they did not intend. Leonard seems to lose confidence in himself, and Sara Selkirk simply becomes rather unlikeable. Nevertheless, all these writers' books are a good read. The final section below takes you on a tour of some of the city centre settings, without giving the game away. It also includes some unexplained hints – to find out why they are there you will have to read the books! Below is the full list.

Peter Lovesey: *The Last Detective* (1991); *Diamond Solitaire* (1998); *The Summons* (1992); *Bloodhounds* (1996); *Upon a Dark Night* (1997); *Do Not Exceed the Stated Dose* (short stories) (1998); *The Vault* (1999); *Diamond Dust* (2002); *The House Sitter* (2003); and *The Secret Hangman* (2007).

Lizbie Brown: *Broken Star* (1992); *Turkey Tracks* (1994); *Shoo-fly* (1998); *Double Wedding Ring* (1999); *Jacob's Ladder* (2000); and *Cat's Cradle* (2001).

Christopher Lee: *The Bath Detective* (1995); *The Killing of Sally Keemer* (1997); *The Killing of Cinderella* (1998).

Morag Joss: *Funeral Music* (1998); *Fearful Symmetry* (1999); and *Fruitful Bodies* (2001).

A walking tour – we do not have murders in Bath, it's bad for the image

This walk begins in the Royal Crescent and ends in Abbey Church Yard.

1. Royal Crescent

We begin our tour with TV's best-known detective, Morse. Nos 15 and 16 make up the Royal Crescent Hotel. In Colin Dexter's book, *Death is Now My Neighbour*, the hotel played a crucial part in a suspect's alibi. The book mentions the manageress, Sara Hickman. Sara actually was the manageress at the time. Not surprisingly, the crescent is mentioned in several of the Bath writers' books, notably *Upon a Dark Night*. In *The Bath Detective*, we only know that the

The consierges wait at the door of the Royal Crescent Hotel *for Morse perhaps?* The author

sinister Montagu James lives in a crescent but everything about the description suggests that it is this one.

Behind the crescent is St James's Square, with its shops, also featured in *Upon a Dark Night.*

From the Crescent can be seen Marlborough Buildings, where there was a real murder in 1828. A manservant, Gilham, killed a fellow servant, Maria Bagnall. He alleged he had found her body after a burglary, but in fact it was proved that she was about to tell their employer that Gilham had been stealing from the house. He killed her to prevent that happening.

The hotel and its grounds played a vital part in Death is Now My Neighbour. The author

A peaceful scene – but also a murder scene in Diamond Dust. The author

Below the Crescent is part of Royal Victoria Park, with the bandstand of 1886. In *Diamond Dust,* a murdered body is found hidden away here, the discovery of which changes Peter Diamond's life forever.

Head along Brock Street to the Circus, noticing the dental surgeries . . .

2. The Circus

The relentless symmetry of the Circus is the inspiration for the title of Morag Joss's book *Fearful Symmetry.* One of the leading characters is the autistic Adele, who is fascinated by the repetitive order of the

The symmetry of the Circus. The author

façade. She lives at No. 31, a clever touch by Morag Joss, for although the circus has thirty-three houses, there is no No. 31 – three houses have their entrances in other streets. To Sara the Circus is claustrophobic. The trees, and the date of their planting are mentioned by Lizbie Brown. Before you leave the Circus, notice Gay Street, where the letting agency in Upon a Dark Night is to be found.

Leave the Circus by Bennett Street and stop outside the entrance to the Assembly Rooms . . .

3. Assembly Rooms

Bennett Street, on the north side of the rooms is where Peter Diamond hides a witness in the house of his superintendent while she is away on holiday. The witness, Anna Walpurgis, does not treat the house with the respect it deserves.

The Assembly Rooms are full of literary connections, such as Dickens, Georgette Heyer and Jane Austen. In *The Last Detective* there is an Antiques Fair here while in *Funeral Music* there is a Health

The Assembly Rooms with Bennett Street beyond. The author

David Price, owner of Woods is the real-life Selsey. The author

Fair, during which a crucial exchange takes place. Lizbie Brown sets a music talk here as an excuse to give some of the history, mentioning the dispute between Herschel and Linley. Lovesey also finds opportunities to slip in snippets of history, while Morag Joss likes to make observations on the city.

Wood's Restaurant, in Alfred Street, on the south side is mentioned by name in Lee's novels, and you may well find the restaurateur, David Price, aka Selsey, in charge – unless it is 'Cheltenham', when he will be at the races.

Take the alleyway near Wood's Restaurant to find . . .

4. Bartlett Street

. . . or Bart's Bazaar, as it appears in *Double Wedding Ring.* This is where Lizbie Brown cheats and alters the layout, but Alfred Place seems to be inspired by St Andrew's Terrace.

Go down Bartlett Street to . . .

5. George Street

This is the street mentioned most often, with its shops and estate agents, restaurants, such as Martini, all of which feature in several

Bartlett Street, home of Bart's Bazaar in Double Wedding Ring. The author

George Street, with its estate agents, bars and restaurants. The author

books. Shades, the wine bar that James Leonard uses when he is not drinking in Wood's has been gone for some time, and is now Sub 13. Also long gone is the bakery in Broad Street, across the road, where Leonard bought his gingerbread men.

Cross in the crossing, turn left and go down into ...

6. Milsom Street

Perhaps the most dramatic event here occurs in *Upon a Dark Night*, when there is a frantic chase through Jolly's. Two other shops that get a mention are Waterstone's and the Savoy Tailor's.

Go down Milsom Street, watching out for Quiet Street on the right hand side ...

7. Quiet Street

Look out for The Kitchen Shop. A good place to purchase a knife, perhaps?

Continue along Quiet Street into ...

Milsom Street. The author

Even a highly respected specialist shop like Kitchens can feature in crime novels. The author

A friendly face in Diamond's favourite bar. The author

8. Queen Square

The bar at the Francis Hotel is one of Diamond's watering holes. When he is called back to work once again for Bath police – in *The Summons* – he refuses and comes straight here. Unfortunately, it is so well known that he likes the bar that he is easily traced to it and picked up.

Turn down Barton Street and head into Beaufort Square to stand at the side of . . .

9. The Theatre Royal

A lethal place to be, if our Bath authors are to be believed. It occurs in *The Killing of Cinderella* (Lee), when the unfortunate murder victim is found hanging from the scenery on stage. An actress is murdered in *Cat's Cradle* (Brown), and Charles Paris has a minor part in a play here, in Simon Brett's *Dead Room Farce*. If you try to follow the walk taken by one of the characters in *Cat's Cradle*, you will find it impossible, proof that Lizbie Brown's Bath is a fictional city.

Retrace your steps to Barton Street and cross into . . .

The Victorian porch to the Theatre Royal. The author

10. Trim Street

One of the perennial puzzles for Lizbie Brown's readers is finding the location of Pierrepont Mews, and 'Martha Washington', Elizabeth Blair's quilt shop above which is the detective agency. Nowhere really

Queen Street and Trim Street, with their picturesque shops referred to in several books. The author

fits the description, but Queen Street, leading out of Trim Street, is a possible option. Melincourt Gallery, in *The Bath Detective* is probably inspired by the Minerva Graphics, especially since a Minerva Gallery appears in the same book, but on Lansdown.

Leave Trim Street by the alleyway at the opposite end from which you entered, turn left, and left again into . . .

11. Old Bond Street

This is another possibility for Pierrepont Mews. There are bow windows.

Regency shop fronts in Old Bond Street. The author

Continue to the end of the block and turn right across Milsom Street into . . .

12. Green Street

Near the far end of Green Street is a little pub named *The Old Green Tree* which Lizbie Brown calls the *Old Green Bush*. Its back room she accurately describes as 'six tiny tables in a room no bigger than the captain's cabin in the Mary Rose'. While some of the menu has changed from the one she lists, you can still get the sausage and special mash. The pub bears no relation to the dreadful *Snake and Ladder* which Morag Joss places in this street, in *Fruitful Bodies*. There

The Old Green Tree *in Green Street.* The author

is a pub elsewhere in Bath which answers the description – it shall remain unnamed. She also has the BITE Festival taking place in the street. BITE is the Bath International Taste Extravaganza and it started in this street, only to move up to Alfred Street. However, thanks to the specialist food shops that have moved in, the BITE festival is back in Green Street.

Continue on down Green Street and turn right, to cross the road to . . .

13. Waitrose Supermarket

All four of our writers must have shares in Waitrose, for it is far and away the most mentioned shop. There is hardly a character who does not nip in here at some time or another for food. The Food Hall at M&S does get into Morag Joss's books, while Peter Lovesey reserves Sainsbury's for the shoplifting scene involving the reprehensible but warm-hearted Ada Shaftsbury in *Upon a Dark Night* and an eventful meeting in *The Secret Hangman.*

Opposite is St Michael's Church, with its side entrance to the crypt visible. It is here that the Bloodhounds meet, in Peter Lovesey's book of the same name. Morag Joss moves St Michael's up the hill to replace St Stephen's in *Funeral Music.* Upstairs in the Podium is the library. A book mentioned by Peter Lovesey is called *In Search of the Perretts.* Its author, the late George Perrett, was delighted to find himself included in the Diamond saga.

Waitrose, where all our detectives do their shopping. The author

Leading away from town is Walcot Street. This is where Michael Z Lewin's family has its detective agency. Many of Lizbie Brown's pubs are fictional, and there is no pub answering the description of the *Princess Amelia* in *Shoofly*. The only pub in Walcot Street is *The Bell*. There are still one or two antique shops left at the far end, where Lovesey has Peg Rainbird, the slightly dodgy antique dealer in *The Vault*.

Walk through the Podium and out the doors at the far end . . .

14. Back of Podium

From here, by looking left, you can see Camden Crescent, where Sara's friend James has a flat. Here too is where the letter bomb goes off, resulting in a fatality.

Turn right and leave by the passageway, turning left to cross . . .

15. Pulteney Bridge

Lizbie Brown thoughtfully provides the reader with a full history of the Pulteney estate in *Shoofly*.

Continue into Argyle Street . . .

16. Argyle Street

This shop was once the Bath branch of Pierre Victoire, which was mentioned several times by Lizbie Brown, under a different name, although the waitress described by her was recognisably a girl who worked there.

Continue into . . .

17. Laura Place

It was here that Louise Shand lived in *Double Wedding Ring*. Look down Great Pulteney Street and imagine both Max Shephard and James Leonard making their way home. Max lived in a flat in Edward Street, while James Leonard lived in a garden flat, with his cat Johnson somewhere near the bridge. Our other detectives lived too far out of town to visit their homes. Sara Selkirk lived at St Catherine's, while Peter Diamond lived first of all on the Wellsway and later at Weston. Elizabeth Blair lives in a village called South Harptree, which does not exist. However, circumstantial evidence suggests that it is Limpley Stoke, and the pub the *Barley Wagon* is probably, in real life, the *Hop Pole*. Wing o' the Hill is her name for Sally i' the Woods, and the American Museum, which overlooks the Limpley Stoke valley, appears in *Turkey Tracks* as the Wedderburn Museum. Other villages such as Twerton, Iford and especially Larkhall make an appearance.

Another pub mentioned by name – Brains Surgery. The author

At Larkhall, Diamond has to meet a witness at the *Brains' Surgery*, while another local the *Larkhall Inn*, figures in the real life case of the Bath Poisoning, mentioned in a previous chapter. At the far end is the Holburne, marking the entrance to Sydney Gardens. Here Diamond's colleague Wigfull had a confrontation with a large pedigree poodle and its irate owner, at the end of which he had retrieved some evidence but failed to discover a body.

Retrace your steps over the bridge and turn left into Grand Parade to admire . . .

18. The River Bank

From here can be seen the weir. This is where a dramatic scene involving the rescue of a boy begins the chain of events which leads to

The Weir, where the rescue of a boy triggers the chain of events in The Last Detective. The author

murder in *The Last Detective*. The Empire Hotel has now been refurbished and converted into upmarket flats, but when Peter Lovesey wrote *The Summons* it was empty and almost derelict. The final denouement takes place there.

Continue along Grand Parade, cross North Parade at the lights and take the gap between the buildings, Duke Street into ...

19. South Parade

The house overlooking the river is the one in which Fanny Burney and the Thrales were staying during the real life events described in Chapter 4. Shortly after this point the Kennet & Avon Canal meets the river. Sara Selkirk often runs along the canal but by and large the canal is not good news. Milo Motion, one of the Bloodhounds, has his narrowboat on the canal, in which a distressing discovery is made and in the same book a body is found under one of the bridges in Sydney Gardens. From here, looking south you can see Beechen Cliff, which features in *Shoofly*, as it does of course in Jane Austen's *Northanger Abbey*, further information that Lizbie Brown is anxious to impart.

Turn right along South Parade and left into Manvers Street to stop outside ...

20. Bath Police Station

All four writers meet here. Apart from the obvious references there are two nice little in-jokes perpetrated by Lovesey and Joss. Peter

Bath Central Police Station. The author

Diamond pokes fun at P D James's fictional detective Dalgleish, while Morag Joss gives DCI Poole a colleague called Inspector Lovesey. Beyond it is the night shelter. The street people that gather there are important to James Leonard in his investigations. Also mentioned in various books at various times are the Comet store, the station, and, south of the river, Widcombe and Lyncombe.

Return up Manvers Street which becomes Pierrepont Street. On your left, marked by a colonnade is Pierrepont Place which leads into . . .

21. Old Orchard

It is tempting to think that this must be Pierrepont Mews especially as there is a patchwork shop. However, this is a case of life following art, for the shop came after the books.

Retrace your steps and continue along Pierrepont Street to . . .

22. North Parade

When Mary Shelley was living in Bath in 1817, she visited an art tutor here – a true story from which Peter Lovesey builds his fictional crime in *The Vault.*

Continue along North Parade, past The Huntsman and Sally Lunn's into ...

23. Abbey Green

Just beyond the archway is a camping shop. For decades this was a fish and chip restaurant known locally as Fishy Evans. In the 1980s there was a real murder here. It is here that Peter Diamond buys two portions of fish and chips at the end of *The Last Detective* in a crucial and touching scene.

Turn right out of Abbey Green into York Street. Turn left and continue along York Street, crossing diagonally at the end into ...

24. Bath Street

The shop on the corner is where Jane Leigh Perrott, Jane Austen's aunt, was alleged to have committed a theft, resulting in a trial at which she was found not guilty. Even today, academics are arguing over whether she was or was not a shoplifter. At the end of Bath Street is the Cross Bath, where a body is found in *The Bath Detective*. The baths attract our writers. Three out of the four have included a death in or near them. So far, no one has found a dead body in the Spa, although a workman fell to his death during the refurbishment of the Cross Bath.

Return up Bath Street and cross under the colonnade into Abbey Church Yard ...

25. Pump Room

Here there are often buskers, as described by Christopher Lee. To him, Bath is a tale of two cities, the rich and the poor. He also comments on all the gossip, with the delightful quote: 'You'd think the whole of Lansdown lived in a telephone box.'

In *Funeral Music*, Sara Selkirk has her return concert in the Pump Room.

Mary Shelley lived a house which was immediately next-door, but was demolished when the Pump Room extension was built. This is now the entrance to the Roman Baths of which there is a wonderful description in *Funeral Music*.

Finally, turn to face ...

26. The Abbey

This is a place of peace for some of our detectives. Diamond often sits here just looking at the building and *The Last Detective* ends here. In *Jacob's Ladder*, the gifted stonemason, Kit Bartram, also looks up at

The Pump Room. The author

Inside, Sara Selkirk held her return concert. The author

The west front of Bath Abbey. The author

the West Front. Normally he comes to the Roman Baths to admire the Gorgon's Head but on this occasion he needs to look up at the angels. By contrast, Sara Selkirk likes the interior with its magnificent fan vaulting.

And so we have travelled through our city of fictional crime, finally drawn, like all our detectives, to its centre.

Bibliography

Primary Sources
Coroners' reports, Bath Record office
Newspapers, Bath Central Library
Chapman Collection, Bath Central Library

Secondary Sources (exluding crime novels – see Chapter 13)

All Roads Lead to France, Andrew Swift, Akeman Press, 2005.

Awash with Ale, Kirsten Elliott & Andrew Swift, Akeman Press, 2004.

Beau Nash, Willard Connely, T Werner Laurie Ltd, 1955.

Bradford on Avon Past & Present, Harold Fassnidge, Ex Libris Press, 1993.

The History of the Somerset Coalfield, C G Downe & A J Warrington, Radstock Museum, 2005.

The Imaginary Autocrat, John Eglin, Profile Books, 2005.

King Mob, Christopher Hibbert, Longman Green, 1958.

Life & Letters at Bath in 18th Century, A Barbeau, William Heinemann, 1904.

The Lost Pubs of Bath, Kirsten Elliott & Andrew Swift, Akeman Press, 2005.

The Murder Club Guide to South West England & Wales, Brian Lane (ed.), Harrap, 1989.

Roman Bath Discovered, Professor Barry Cunliffe, Tempus, 2000.

The Search for the Source of the Nile: Correspondence between Captain Richard Burton, Captain John Speke and others, Quentin Keynes (ed.) and Donald Young, The Roxburghe Club, 1988.

The Temple of Julis Milova of Bath, II, Barry Cunliffe.

Walks Through Bath, Pierce Egen, 1819.

Index